D0645512

Dedicated to the life of

Jim Rohn

whose legacy of inspiration continues to fuel the hearts of those who aspire to the extraordinary.

Also by the Author

Become the Person You Dream of Being
Dating the Dream
Escape to Prosperity
Give Your Life a Success Makeover
Go and Be Successful
FUEL: The Energy You Need To Succeed

Contents

Gratitudes

I want to thank the team of entrepreneurs (The FUEL Group) that met with me every week. Many of your insights and experiences became a catalyst for me writing *FUEL 2*. Keep going for it, team. The world becomes better with every dream that you bring into reality. Thanks to Greg and Amy Albertyn for being our generous hosts.

Special thanks to Bill Schulz of *IMA Design*. Not only does your environmental architecture make the world aesthetically pleasing, your friendship and example is monumentally inspiring to me. It's great being on the journey with you.

Many thanks to Patrick and Laarni Kelly for the dedicated way that you have contributed to Ellie and me continuing our calling of positively impacting the lives of others.

Enormous appreciation to my editors and proof readers. Knowing that I have your talents working on my writing projects gives me much peace of mind.

Additional thanks to Peter McGowan, Mike Foster, Julie McDougal and everyone at PlainJoe Studios who contribute their experience and talent to my efforts to communicate inspiration. I value your friendship as well as your expertise.

To Mark Lydell, thanks for your excellence in taking great photos of a moving target in low light conditions!

To Ira and Samuel Lippke, Scott McAlvany, and Anne Hjelle whose lives exemplify faith and courage. Thanks for your contributions to this book.

To everyone at my favorite coffee and tea house who kept me going with hot drinks and an engaging atmosphere as I wrote this book. To Manager Tim and your awesome baristas, Jai, Nick, Natalie, Wes, Phil, Adrienne, Timmy Dean, Davey and Megan—you make the world a happier place, one cup at a time.

Utmost thanks to Ellie and our sons, David and Zack. We are a great team. Always will be! Never underestimate the impact of your love and thoughtful words.

To those who read my books, I am sincerely grateful for you. It is your desire to grow and do something extraordinary with your lives that affords me the privilege to be an author. May the words I write help you, in some way, to achieve your dreams.

Finally, to all the leaders around the world who invite me to speak to your wonderful people, I am forever indebted. Thank you for never giving up. Even in the face of adverse conditions, you have maintained your calling to lead people and provide for them an opportunity to grow. You are the heroes in my life. It's an honor to serve you.

Introduction

He fed his spirit with the bread of books.
Edwin Markham

My eighteen year old son is a hard working student and like most students, his net worth is the sum total of coins in his car's cup holder! When he came home from school today, I wanted to say "I love you, son" in a practical way. So I took his car to the local fuel station and paid for a tank of gas. As the pump refilled the car, I started wondering how many times I have replenished the fuel of various vehicles in my thirty plus years of driving. I did a quick calculation and determined that I must have "filled up the tank" at least three thousand times. That's three thousand times of going back for more fuel whenever I was running low.

There have been times when I have been disconcerted by the price of fuel. There have even been occasions when I have only had the money to move the needle on the fuel gauge a hair above empty. Sometimes I have barely made it to the refilling station before running out. But for all the hassles, I have always been at peace with the reality that my vehicle needs energy refills to keep going.

I like what fuel helps me accomplish. My gratefulness for it overrides the guilt of creating a carbon footprint (sorry!). You see, most places I need to travel are not downhill all the way or just around the corner. There are many long stretches and uphill climbs in my journeys. Yet, they are not problematic because fuel powers me through them. So rain, hail or sunshine never gets in the way of me stopping to refuel my vehicle. And I am always willing to pay for that fuel.

For the same reason, I highly value the practice of reading inspirational books and listening to inspiring speakers. I am an avid goal setter and dream achiever. The bigger the goal, the more inspiration I need to accomplish it. So refueling my mind is not something I do when I get a spare moment. What mover and shaker has spare moments? Inspiring my mind is not a luxury. Inspiration is a necessity. It keeps me bold and effective in overcoming the obstacles between me and my goals. So I regularly fill up with inspiring words. Although the stimulation of today's words will wear off as surely as the stimulating effects of this morning's coffee will wear off by lunch time, even so, do we stop drinking coffee?!

Behavioral scientists say that humans get psychologically tired. Anyone who has tried to lose weight has probably heard someone say that "diets don't work." The reality is that diets do work in causing weight loss; it's just that people become psychologically weary of sticking to them. It's quite apparent that our minds just simply cannot go the distance on one tank of inspiration. Overcoming psychological fatigue is essential to going the distance to reaching our dreams. So we need to fill up again and again. I am not just saying that because I am an author. I, too, need to constantly fill up on motivating thoughts to overcome obstacles in my journey. There have been so many times when reading a book has replaced my depressing thoughts with the mental energy to press on to a victory.

> Overcoming psychological fatigue is essential to going the distance to reaching our dreams.

I have also learned that motivational books are not meant to be treasure maps. Too many people approach a book with the hope that it will contain the elusive secret to success. Frankly, the location of success is not a secret. It's just on the other side of a resolute effort. More often than not, what is needed to make that effort is just some fresh juice that takes us from being psychologically tired, to being psychologically energized. This book is not about unlocking the daVinci code of success. Rather, it is inspirational fuel for your spirit; it is success propellant.

My previous book *FUEL: The Energy You Need to Succeed* resonated so much with people that I have followed it up with *FUEL 2: Keeping You and Your Team Fired Up!* It continues the theme that becoming successful is less about avoiding obstacles and more about having the fuel to push through obstacles. I want to load you up with enough fuel for you and your team to burst through to the next level. How high can you go? I don't know. But I do know that it's higher than where you are today. Better days are ahead for those who push on to claim them. The key factors in your pace will be what you think about and where those thoughts are taking you.

If I can convey any sense of authority on the subject of psychological fuel, it's not because I have it all together. It's because I know what it is like to be stopped on the side of life's road having run out of inspiration to go on. What I offer you is what I have discovered re-energizes the human spirit in such times. Somewhere along my journey, someone introduced me to the power of reading for inspiration and energy. Without a doubt, reading has been a major key in getting me fired up to do the work that it takes to succeed. And staying fired up requires the habit of regularly topping up. Last month's fuel injection has already been spent.

So, as I did for my son today, let me fill your tank anew so that you can keep pressing on towards that next level of achievement. Regardless of where we are at in the journey, we are on this journey together. Let's fill up so that we can power through our challenges and meet with the success that is our reward for having done so.

Wes Beavis

1. Responsibility

Success on any major scale requires you to accept
responsibility. In the final analysis, the one quality
that all successful people have is the ability
to take on responsibility.
Michael Korda

When the 2004 tsunami hit Indonesia, the lives
of brothers Ira and Samuel Lippke and their friend
Scott McAlvany were forever changed. I first met Ira
at a photo shoot in Long Beach, California, in 1999.
Ira and his brother, Samuel, are professional photog-
raphers who are brilliant in their ability to capture life
in a photograph. Although they are younger than I,
what they did in the wake of the tsunami's devas-
tation of Indonesia makes them my heroes. What
started for them as a surfing vacation, ended with
them saving countless lives amidst one of the greatest
natural disasters of our lifetime.

Up until the tsunami hit, Ira, Samuel and Scott

had divided their days teaching in a local orphanage and surfing the world class waves at the base of the Ulawatu Cliffs. When news broke that a tsunami had hit Sumatra, two islands from their location, they decided to gather as many medical supplies as they could and travel to the epicenter, Banda Aceh.

But flying to Banda Aceh proved to be quite a challenging task in itself. For various reasons, the government had long closed the doors to Western involvement in the area. The scope of the tsunami damage was largely unknown at that point and so the closed door policy remained. Yet, the Lippke brothers, Ira and Samuel, and their friend Scott kept trying to find a way in. They were sent from one person to another, leading all the way to the governor of Sumatra who, after making them sign liability waivers, gave them permission to enter the region. So lugging all their equipment and supplies to the air force base, they boarded the next plane to the region. Finding somewhere to sit in the fuselage amidst the food supplies, diesel fuel, and soldiers, they headed to a place from which they would never return the same.

When the plane landed in Banda Aceh, they were greeted with the stench of death and the debris of disaster. Most every building near the beach had been turned into a pile of rubble and bodies. The dead far outnumbered the living. In every direction there were bodies, burned and bloated. The air was putrefied by broken sewer pipes and rotting flesh in the humid heat. Those alive were in a daze of shock looking for missing family. The disaster level was yet to be fully realized by the rest of the world. When Ira,

Samuel, and Scott arrived, there was barely any aid work happening at all. They were among the first "outsiders" to the region. With the help of their Indonesian translator, Rollie, they got to work.

There were few medical workers. The local hospital was destroyed, along with the lives of its doctors and nurses. Still, thousands of injured and dying were being brought to a makeshift hospital. For four straight days, the guys raced against time, cutting out septic infections from wounds, helping with surgeries and amputations, and hauling bodies away to stem the spread of disease. The sick and injured waited for days only to be treated with limited medication and no anesthetic.

On the fifth day, the doors to the region were opened and additional help from all over the world started to arrive. By this time, thoroughly exhausted, Ira, Samuel and Scott handed over the reins to trained aid workers and boarded a flight home. Lives had been transformed—including their own.

You may be thinking how fortunate that three young doctors were near the region when the tsunami struck. But that is just the point. Ira, Samuel and Scott had no medical qualifications at all. They were surfers whose professional expertise lay in photography and business, not disaster relief. An aid agency wouldn't have considered them to be part of a first responder's team, at least not for providing medical aid. And yet, for four days, while aid agencies were trying to gain

> Leadership is more about taking responsibility than having leadership qualifications.

access to the area, these brazen surfers managed to talk their way into a restricted region and help save lives that would have been lost without their efforts.

Ira, Samuel and Scott became examples of the fact that becoming a leader is more about taking responsibility than having leadership qualifications. Leadership doesn't start in the head; leadership starts in the heart. Regardless of their lack of resources and medical qualifications, they initiated a mission of restoring hope and order no matter how bleak or overwhelming the circumstances.

Samuel, Scott & Ira

On December 26th, 2004, an undersea megathrust earthquake caused coastal tsunamis that killed nearly 230,000 people in fourteen countries.

Vastly under-resourced and without being asked, three surfers thrust themselves into the chaos. They took responsibility for the needs of the people until help arrived five days later.

Samuel, Scott, Rollie(translator) and Ira, boarding the C-130 cargo plane. Heading home after having made a difference.

photos provided courtesy of www.iralippkestudios.com

If you want to make a positive difference in the world, it starts with taking responsibility for bringing it about. It doesn't matter how inadequate you might feel or how many obstacles are in your way. Increase your impact by increasing your responsibility. Don't wait for others to make the difference. If you decide that the responsibility for making the future better is 100% yours, then you are the captain of your future.

I heard a commentator say recently, "Your life is the way that it is because you have made it that way." When I first heard it, I thought it was totally insensitive to those who have had unfortunate things happen to them. Not everyone has had the benefit of a functional family upbringing. Many people have been unfairly treated and their lives reflect it. Yet, the more I thought about it, the more I realize that it is a powerful statement that can liberate a person to build a better life.

> "Action springs not from thought, but from a readiness for responsibility."
>
> Dietrich Bonhoeffer

You see, if you take full responsibility for who you are today, then you have full authority to change yourself. If you attribute elements of who you are to bad conditions, then you will need certain favorable conditions in order to change into something better. Seeing yourself as the product of circumstances means you have surrendered a portion of your development to circumstances. And since we can't always control our circumstances, we are left at the mercy of favorable circumstances in order to change for the better. So don't blame your "bad" parts on someone or something else because that gives those negative factors power to form your future as well.

Instead, be the captain of your life and your circumstances. Regardless of how tough the conditions may be, take responsibility for being fired up. Don't be like the rest of the population that needs things to be favorable before becoming fired up. Things can and will go wrong. When things on the space rocket Apollo 13 went horribly wrong, astronaut Jim Lovell famously declared, "Houston, we have a problem." He didn't follow it up by grumbling, "Man, I didn't sign up for this!" Not at all. He was the captain by choice and by commitment. He continued to take full responsibility for the flight and the safety of his crew, especially in the face of problems.

Leadership expert, John Maxwell, determined that only two percent of the population are initiators of change. The rest are either gradual adopters of change or resistors to change. So what do you have to do to become part of the two percent of initiators? Simply decide to become one! Put yourself in that category. It doesn't matter if you are qualified or not. Just initiate something positive. Define yourself as an initiator—someone who determines the temperature rather than responds to the temperature.

Initiate progress for you and your team. Be responsible for a fired up atmosphere whether you feel qualified or not. Ira, Samuel and Scott were not "medically qualified" for the responsibility of helping the tsunami ravaged people of Banda Aceh. But they qualified themselves as being responsible for helping to restore hope and order. They focused not on what they didn't have, but focused on what they did have; the heart to make a positive difference. As a result, they helped to save the lives of hundreds, possibly thousands, of people.

Do you have the heart to make a positive difference? Then regardless of how inadequate you might feel or how many obstacles are in your way, be 100% responsible for making positive change for your life and for the lives of your team. Build a reputation as someone who takes responsibility. It is the foundation upon which success is built.

Now to the How to: **Responsibility**

1. From this day forward classify yourself as a natural responsibility taker. Take pride in being responsible.

2. Hold yourself solely responsible for what your life has become up to this point. Don't blame anyone or anything else for your position in life. If you take full responsibility for your past, you have full authority to create your future.

3. Think of someone you admire for the quality of "taking responsibility." Invite them out for a meal. You be responsible for paying! Talk about the subject of responsibility and ask them what motivates them to be responsible. Imitate their qualities.

4. Ask your leaders for more responsibility and deliver results, not excuses.

Quick FUEL: **Responsibility**

You are always 100% in control and have 100% responsibility for everything that has occurred in your life as a result of your actions or inactions. *Darren Hardy*

The best years of your life are the ones in which you decide your problems are your own. You do not blame them on your mother, the ecology, or the president. You realize that you control your own destiny. *Albert Ellis*

Not being able to do everything is no excuse for not doing everything you can. *Ashleigh Brilliant*

You are not responsible for the programming you picked up in childhood. However, as an adult, you are one hundred percent responsible for fixing it. *Ken Keyes, Jr.*

Action springs not from thought, but from a readiness for responsibility. *Dietrich Bonhoeffer*

All blame is a waste of time. No matter how much fault you find with another, and regardless of how much you blame him, it will not change you. *Wayne Dyer*

Excuses are the cradles in which failure lulls us to sleep. *Anon*

"I must do something" always solves more problems than "Something must be done." *Anon*

It is easy to dodge our responsibilities, but we cannot dodge the consequences of dodging our responsibilities. *Josiah Charles Stamp*

The willingness to accept responsibility for one's own life is the source from which self-respect springs. *Joan Didion*

Success Workshop: Responsibility

1. Do you assume responsibility quickly or do you need to be motivated? Rate yourself on the following scale.

Need to be motivated   Assume quickly

2. Of the people you know, who is a good example of someone who is quick to assume responsibility?

_____

In what ways has taking responsibility made their life better than yours?

_____

_____

3. Give three reasons why you struggle with taking responsibility.

_____

_____

_____

4. Complete the following sentences:
If I took more responsibility in doing _____
_____ then I would enjoy more of
_____.

If people notice me taking more responsibility for
_____ I would then be given more
_____.

5. I commit to increasing my responsibility for the following things in my life:

A. _____

B. _____

C. _____

The people in my team increase their responsibility when I concentrate on doing the following:

_____

2. Faith

Faith is the art of holding on to things
your reason has once accepted in spite
of your changing moods.
C.S. Lewis

Even to save itself, a caterpillar cannot jump one millimeter off the ground. If you were to examine the caterpillar's form and behavior, you would correctly assume a fairly mundane future for this little creature. Yet, that would be a mistake. For while everything about the caterpillar's current appearance and function seems uninspiring, there's something transformational within the caterpillar. Contained within the caterpillar's DNA is the mechanism to transform it into a butterfly. So powerful is this transformation that it's hard to believe that the butterfly started out as a humble caterpillar in the first place. We have this same transformational power within us. Faith is the mechanism that starts our transformation.

No one is born successful. People become successful by believing that their life can be transformed into something better and they support that belief with actions. That's what faith is: Believing that a better life is possible, way before you see any evidence of such and *acting on that belief*. It is this faith which compels a person to enter the cocoon of personal transformation. I have never known a person to succeed without first having faith that they are born to become successful.

You might have convinced yourself that certain things are impossible. To a plodding caterpillar restricted to crawling, becoming a beautiful butterfly that is free to fly wherever it pleases seems impossible. But not only is it possible, it is meant to happen. Likewise your success is not only possible but it is meant to happen. The transformation process awaits your faith to get it started. You must believe it in your heart first. As Friedrich von Schlegel said, "In life every great enterprise begins with and takes its first step forward in faith."

Faith has two stages—the birth stage and the development stage. The birth stage can take place in a very short time frame. Faith is birthed in a person the moment they believe something better is possible. Once faith is birthed, then it is a case of strengthening that fledgling faith over a lifetime. In the words of J.O. Fraser, "Faith is like a muscle which grows stronger and stronger with use, rather than rubber, which weakens when it is stretched."

It's not enough to just "have faith"—you must be committed to increasing and strengthening your faith. It's not a "set and forget" process. Be assured, every challenging situation, rejection, and discouragement will be working to erode your faith just as you are working to increase it. So it's not enough to start believing, you need to re believe everyday and *act* on that belief in order to make your faith stronger. There is a reason why they say, "Keep the faith," because it's possible to lose it.

Of course, it makes a world of difference in your ability to produce faith when what you are having faith in, is faith-worthy. As the old saying goes: "It's better to have weak faith in a strong bridge than to have strong faith in a weak bridge." To have bold faith that, if all else fails, a rich uncle is going to rescue you, may be a case of misplaced faith. But to have bold faith in your ability to improve and make life better is a case of well placed faith. Indeed you have the capacity to improve, however good or bad your situation may be.

Faith is the unifying factor in a team. There has to be a common belief that keeps people bonded and headed in the same direction. Groups fall apart when people lose faith. Your group, team or organization will only be as strong as people's absolute conviction that what you are collectively involved in is working. In any team, it doesn't matter who calls themselves the leader, people follow the person who has the most faith in themselves, their product and the results to prove

> "You have to decide, right here and right now, whether to live your life in fear or faith."
> Barbara Geraghty

their faith has not been misplaced. So if you want to become a leader, you don't have to be voted in or be promoted in. You are the leader by having the most faith in your product, service and the results that prove it. Your team will naturally look to you and mimic you, regardless of your title.

If you are the leader and your faith is sinking, you must raise it again. You may be able to coast for a little while as you sort yourself out but people are intuitive. After a while, your followers can sense that your faith tank is empty. What do followers do? They follow! So if you are heading down Doubt Street, they're going to follow you, losing heart along the way. Without a common faith that holds people together, the people scatter. Some will quit while others look for another leader. Don't let this happen. If you find your faith languishing, get together with other faith-filled leaders and borrow some of their faith until you resuscitate yours.

How do you build faith in your team? Your first step is to talk about it. Make faith a team issue.

People want to have faith. There is a proclivity within humans to want the future to be better, so you don't have to sell them on the idea of having faith. Teach them the nuances of birthing and developing faith. What was it that caused you first to believe? How have you developed your faith?

Success comes to those who operate under the leadership of faith rather than feelings.

Share your story. Provide an opportunity for others in your team to share their story. Most people are just needing permission and encouragement to get started. When they hear your story and the experience of others, they will realize that faith is just a decision away.

Your team also needs to know that it's okay to struggle with faith. They need to know that it is normal to have a faith crisis every so often. From time to time we wonder if we are doomed to being a caterpillar spending the rest of our lives watching butterflies do their thing! There are days when our faith gets clobbered by the circumstances or is just plain tired. A good leader won't condemn people for having an occasional faith-crisis, but a good leader won't give permission for people to wallow there. When faith is weak, feelings (usually bad ones) are strong. Success comes to those who operate under the leadership of faith rather than feelings. So develop a team ethos of building faith in each other, your product or service.

Have faith meetings. Individual faith will flourish where collective faith gathers. You don't need to be religious to have a faith meeting. Faith is bigger than religion. Faith is believing that the future can be better than the present and then *acting on it*. Or as W.T. Purkiser says, "Faith is more than thinking something is true. Faith is thinking that it is true to the extent that we act on it." So have team faith parties, faith picnics, and faith programs. Celebrate the birth of faith in the individual and celebrate the building of faith in the team and its objectives. The first step to every success starts with a leap of faith.

Now to the How to: Faith

1. Commit to memory this statement, "Faith is acting on my beliefs."

2. Set your daily guidance system to be led by your faith and not your feelings.

3. Make a list of all of your faith-driven actions and give priority to those actions over feeling-driven actions.

4. Get together with team partners and compare faith steps and strategies. Spur each other on to being loyal to one's faith-driven actions.

Quick FUEL: Faith

Faith is to believe what you do not yet see; the reward for this faith is to see what you believe.
St. Augustine

You block your dream when you allow your fear to grow bigger than your faith. *Mary Manin Morrissey*

Faith is like electricity. You can't see it, but you can see the light. *Anon*

A fellow shouldn't abandon his faith when it weakens, any more than he'd throw away a suit because it needs pressing. *Frank A. Clark*

Faith fuels will power—doubt produces won't power. *Anon*

Faith is not a commodity like coffee or toothpaste. It is more like a tree. It grows. *David Winter*

Faith is continuing to run the race, assured that you will get your second wind. *William A. Ward*

I would rather err on the side of faith than on the side of doubt. *Robert Schuller*

Faith is not belief. Belief is passive. Faith is active. *Edith Hamilton*

Faith is not something to grasp, it is a state to grow into. *Mahatma Gandhi*

Faith makes things possible, not easy. *Anon*

Success Workshop: Faith

1. Does adding actions to your beliefs come easily to you or do you struggle with having faith? Rate yourself on the following scale.

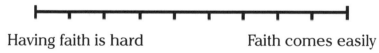

Having faith is hard   Faith comes easily

2. What are the three main reasons that stop me from taking leaps of faith?

_____

_____

                                                    •
_____

3. The biggest leap of faith I ever took was:

_____

4. Who is someone you admire for their faith?

_____

How does their faith show in their life?

_____

_____

5. If you could raise your faith in one area, what would that be?

_____

How could having greater faith in this area help you to succeed?

_____

_____

3. Vision

There is no more powerful engine driving an
organization toward excellence and long-range
success than an attractive, worthwhile, achievable
vision for the future, widely shared.
Burt Nanus

In 2005, I was packing my bag to go to Cairo, Egypt. At the last minute, I decided to switch to a smaller bag and quickly dumped all the contents from one bag into another. In the process, I didn't notice that my glasses had fallen onto the bed instead of into the bag. I rushed off to the airport and boarded a plane not realizing that all I had separating me from legal blindness were my contacts—two flimsy pieces of plastic suctioned onto my eyeballs. Hours into the flight, I decided to take out my contacts and switch over to my glasses, which by that time were four thousand miles away.

Realizing my error, I figured that, short of trying

to find an optometrist in Cairo, I would just cope with wearing my contacts all of the time. This strategy sufficed to get me through a week of meetings and speaking appointments until the final night. Without warning, I was struck with the vulnerabilities of my blindness!

On the final night, my hosts took me to the midnight market place which was across the road from the University of Cairo. It was a hive of exciting activity and nightlife. It seemed like the population of Egypt all converged upon this one location. The markets were thriving with merchants and buyers, restaurants and music. The hot evening air was filled with the aroma of Middle Eastern cuisine and the smoke from hundreds of tobacco pipes. The dust and diesel fumes from a myriad of busses, cars and taxis thickened the air. It would not have been a problem, had I been wearing my glasses! But having already worn my contacts for eighteen hours that day, my eyeballs literally shutdown. The contact lenses lost all of their moisture and had become glued to the surface of my eyes. I blinked and could not open my eyelids. I was effectively rendered blind.

> People lack personal power because they don't have a clear vision of where they are headed.

Our fun plans for the night were abruptly changed to trying to locate a medical pharmacy that would be open at 1AM in the morning. Had I needed a gold necklace or a hand-woven rug, I would have been in the perfect place. But I needed some special eye drops that would get my eyes working again.

I had heard the saying, "Where there is no vision, the people perish." I remember feeling like I was going to personally test the validity of that principle! Eventually, we found a place that was able to provide a remedy. I was so relieved to have my eyesight back.

Upon returning home to Los Angeles, I immediately booked an appointment with an eye surgeon to have my eyes permanently laser corrected. I had been thinking about having the surgery for years. That stressful night in Cairo was just the motivation I needed! I never wanted to feel that vulnerable again. Thankfully, the surgery worked brilliantly and I have had pristine vision ever since.

There is something about lacking clear vision— not knowing where you're headed in life—that makes you feel vulnerable. Many people lack personal power because they don't have a clear vision of where they are headed. There's nothing like a clear desirable destination that coerces people to put themselves firmly in drive.

Someone once quipped, "If you don't know where you are going, you will end up someplace else!" And that someplace else is not all that special. My dad passed away twenty-five years ago but I remember him telling me as if it were yesterday, "Son, if you aim at nothing, that's what you will get every time!"

The next step, after making the decision to be responsible for your future and to strengthen your faith, is to choose an inspiring destination at which you can aim. In some circles, this is called having a dream. A dream is simply the desire for something, of which the attainment, first starts in your imagination. Indeed, nothing splendid is ever achieved by accident. Great achievements start as great dreams.

Recently, I had lunch with Motocross World Champion, Greg Albertyn. He was first inspired to become the world champion when he was twelve years old. For years, the vision of becoming the "best of the best" motivated him to keep going when the broken bones, lonely times, and disappointments tempted him to quit. He started as a kid growing up in South Africa—not exactly the motocross capital of the world—and ended up beating Europe and America's finest riders to become the world champion. Winning required immense effort, but it was Greg's clear vision for winning that fueled his effort.

The purpose of a dream is to get you excited enough that you spring into action. I have never heard anyone say, "I made it all the way to the top propelled by a lukewarm inclination!" You need something more potent than that to get you jumping out of bed in the morning and charging through a field of rejections without losing enthusiasm! As Robert Kriegel once said, "The key is to have a dream that inspires us to go beyond our limits."

Some people have a vision for finding an easy way to succeed. That's not a vision—that's wishful thinking! There's nothing easy about succeeding. Those that look for the "easy way" are often tempted to take shortcuts that inevitably lead them into dead end streets having to start over again. The key is not finding an easy way to succeed, but establishing a vision so compelling that you achieve your dream regardless of the hardships in the way. A vision for a destination that excites you is the key to staying fired up when otherwise you would flame out.

I wish I could tell you that every one of my bodacious dreams has become a reality. Frankly, they haven't. The pile of my broken dreams is as tall as a mountain. Some dreams just never materialize. But one thing is for sure, my monumental achievements all started with a dream in the first place. As I have matured in understanding the success journey, I've become more draconian towards my dreams. If they no longer inspire me, I toss them overboard. A dream that has lost its motivational power becomes the opposite—an obligation rather than an inspiration. Cut it loose. If it doesn't fire you up, then fire it! It's done its job. It's got you out of bed more times than otherwise. But if it no longer causes you to smile every time you think of it, then get yourself a fresh dream.

Once you decide on an inspiring destination, keep it clearly before you. Some people put a picture of their dream as the wallpaper of their computer screen or cell phone. Others put a photo of their dream on their refrigerator or office desk.

My friends, Ray and his wife Judi, own a wealth management company. They have several rooms which are purpose designated for meetings with clients. But instead of the rooms being deco-rated in the usual professional décor, Ray and Judi themed each room to represent different visions that people might have for their future. One room is the tropical island set. When you walk into the room, you feel like you have walked onto a beach in the tropics. The walls are covered with beach wallpaper. There's a bamboo drink cabana in the room, palm trees, and even beach toys. Being in the room makes you feel like you are on vacation. All that's missing is sand on the floor. Ray is probably trying to figure out how to make that happen too! Walk into another room and you feel like you have walked into a Paris café. Another room and you find yourself somewhere in Asia. Ray and Judi have gone to great lengths to make the décor of each room inspire and elevate the vision of their clients.

> "Great vision comes from being in a great community."
>
> Dave Gibbons

I heard author and advocate for liquid leadership, Dave Gibbons, say recently, "Great vision comes from being in a great community." If you are lacking vision, it could be that you are not keeping good company. Keeping yourself fired up is easier when you are surrounded by fired up visionary people. If the people that you hang around have a great vision for their lives, the same fervor for the future will get into your system.

It's paramount if you are leading a team to keep the vision constantly before your team. People either forget the vision or the mundane stuff of life covers it up. A team vision has a unifying effect on the team. It has an excitement factor to it. What is your team vision? How often do you celebrate it? Theodore Hesburgh said, "The very essence of leadership is that you have a vision. It's got to be a vision you articulate clearly and forcefully on every occasion. You can't blow an uncertain trumpet."

I developed an exercise that helps me keep a clear focus on my vision. Every night before I go to sleep, I write out my dream in what I call my *Success Journal*. Even though I have already written out my dream the night before and the night before that, I write it down again. I find that not reiterating my dream on a daily basis causes me to lose focus. The dream gets fuzzy and it loses its power to influence. Dreams are hard to achieve when they become blurry. Writing down my dream every night keeps me from losing my focus. Start the practice of writing down your vision every day and see the influence it has on keeping you and your team fired up.

The Great Sphinx of Giza near Cairo, Egypt, is the largest and oldest monumental sculpture standing in the world today. Built about 4553 years ago, it began with one person having a vision!

Now to the How to: *Vision*

1. Sort out from the myriad of dreams "the one thing" that you want more than anything else. Declare that as your vision.

2. Articulate your vision in one sentence that you can memorize.

3. Create a tangible representation of that vision, such as a photo or laminated description, as a reminder of that for which you are aiming.

4. Find an accountability partner with whom you can share each other's visions and hold each other accountable.

5. Organize a vision party with your team. Celebrate the possibilities and give honor to each person's vision for their future.

6. As a team leader, articulate the team vision each time you get together.

Quick FUEL: Vision

We lift ourselves by our thought. We climb upon our vision of ourselves. If you want to enlarge your life, you must first enlarge your thought of it and of yourself. Hold the ideal of yourself as you long to be, always everywhere. *Orison Swett Marden*

Formulate and stamp indelibly on your mind a mental picture of yourself as succeeding. Hold this picture tenaciously. Never permit it to fade. Your mind will seek to develop the picture.
Norman Vincent Peale

Dissatisfaction and discouragement are not caused by the absence of things but the absence of vision.
Anon

A rock pile ceases to be a rock pile the moment a single man contemplates it, bearing within him the image of a cathedral. *Antoine De Saint-Exupery*

A leader has the vision and conviction that a dream can be achieved. He inspires the power and energy to get it done. *Ralph Lauren*

The future belongs to those who see possibilities before they become obvious. *John Scully*

When you have vision it affects your attitude. Your attitude is optimistic rather than pessimistic.
Charles R. Swindoll

Vision is the art of seeing the invisible.
Jonathan Swift

Life is filled with decisive moments when you have to trade one thing for another. A visionary will always trade up—never down. *Barbara Geraghty*

Dreams are extremely important. You can not do it unless you can imagine it. *George Lucas*

The trouble with not having a goal is that you can spend your life running up and down the field and never scoring. *Bill Copeland*

Success Workshop: Vision

1. How clear is your vision for your future? Rate yourself on the following scale.

Fuzzy   Crystal clear

2. The vision I have for my future can be summed up in the following sentence:

_____

3. My team vision can be summed up by the following sentence:

_____

_____

4. The following three things get in the way and stop me from focusing on my vision:

_____

_____

_____

5. In the following ways, my life will change for the better when I achieve my vision for the future:

_____

_____

_____

6. Name two people in your life that you admire for having a clear vision for their future.

_____ and _____

In what way can you imitate them?

_____

_____

4. Passion

A strong passion for any object will ensure success,
for the desire of the end will point out the means.
William Hazlitt

Where does passion come from? Are some
people more naturally passionate than others? Can
you succeed without passion?

Everyone is born with the ability to be
passionate. Every baby I have known has an inborn
ability to holler up a storm when they were hungry or
they needed some dry pants. It doesn't matter what
time of the day or night, that little bundle of joy will
break every noise abatement code with passionate
pleas to have their needs met.

Passion is the ability to be self-driven towards
achieving a desired result. It is a natural tendency that
everyone has and you can't succeed without it.

You don't lose passion in as much as it just gets buried under a pile of other stuff. So when you see someone lacking passion, it's not because they have lost the ability to be passionate. Mostly, it's just a case of people being overcome by other things and their passion is shut out of the game.

Every one of us knows highly passionate people, and to be truthful, some of these people demonstrate such a high level of passion that we feel completely boring by comparison. Do we need to start jumping out of planes and wrestling crocodiles to release the passion within us? Not necessarily. How much passion do you need in order to be successful? As much as you can muster. Passion for what you do is essential to being successful at it. Passion attracts people, vision galvanizes them, and the experience of ongoing value retains them.

Passion displays itself differently in each personality. I know some very conservative people whose passion for what they do runs deep and strong and they have the results to prove it. Passion is not about being flamboyant. Don't get sidetracked thinking you have to become like an infomercial pitchman in order to succeed. It's not a question of becoming like another person, but about you burning hotter for your cause. As E.M. Forster said, "One person with passion is better than forty people merely interested."

Is it possible that some people are naturally more inclined to be passionate than others? In other words, are they born with a double portion of passion? If this were true, then all of us have a very good excuse for our lack of it. We could simply relegate ourselves to the percentile of the population that is not "naturally" passionate, and that would be our excuse. The trouble is that no one really knows whether passion is the product of nature or nurture. Psychologists have been debating the nature versus nurture argument for years.

My conclusion is based on experiential and observational evidence: People with passion succeed more than those without it, and everyone can increase their level of enthusiasm if they make it their intention to do so. So regardless of what level of enthusiasm you think you were born with, you have the potential and the need

> Passion attracts people, vision galvanizes them, and the experience of ongoing value retains them.

to increase it. Passion is a success magnet. Here are some catalysts for stirring up passion.

Increase passion by life reorganization

We are born with the ability to be passionate. But it's easy for our passion to be squelched by the concerns of life. People think that they don't have passion, when it's really a case of their passions have no place to rise up and breathe. Passions stay submerged beneath a heavy layer of other things. If you want to feel the passion, you have to create room for it to rise. Creating room, or what I call margins, for passions to rise is a key to feeling passionate again.

One of the pitfalls of modern society is that people live right to the edges of their lives. Margins are no longer created much less protected. Every spare moment and dollar is utilized and tapped for its potential, often on noble things. Sometimes people over extend themselves "for the cause." But the first casualty of our over-extension is our passion. One day we wake up and wonder where our passion went. We feel zestless and uninspired, and think that the solution to our energy shortfall will be found in "doing something else." We forsake our path to "look for something better." But all along our passion didn't up and leave—it just got buried. And without a margin through which to come up for air, it stays buried.

Success in life is about managing our lives. Maxing out your every waking moment with productivity without creating a space for your spirit to breathe will leave your spirit drained. The state of your spirit governs the level of your passion. S. Truett Cathy, founder of Chick-fil-A restaurants, mandates that all of his restaurants close on Sunday. Wall Street would criticize him for opportunity losses to his store profits. For a restaurant to be closed for 50% of the weekend would seem to be business suicide. Yet, S. Truett Cathy didn't like working on Sundays. He liked having a solid day of rest from business. It refreshed his spirit and he figured that his restaurant staff deserved the same break. Despite the one day a week closure, Chick-fil-A's profitability is the envy of many of their competitors and as someone quipped, "Being closed on Sunday makes their chicken sandwich taste so good on Mondays!"

Having passion is a key to being successful at what we do. But you have to create space in your life for your passion to breathe. As I write, I realize that anyone looking for validation to be a slacker, will love what I have written. I can hear you telling your team associates, "Hey, I'm not working right now because

Wes Beavis told me I should give CPR to my passion!"
So I need to clarify that this section on margins is
specifically for productive people who are discover-
ing that their passion is waning—not for people looking to validate their lack of productivity!

In the business world, failing businesses are
saved every day through a process called re-organization. It's a wonderful process because it saves
people from losing their
jobs, saves towns from being
devastated and rescues the
value of iconic brands being
lost forever. I wish we could
borrow that concept for our
own personal lives, because
oftentimes, all we need is a

> "If you want to be successful,
> don't look for something
> better, become better at
> what you do and success
> will find you."
> Charlie "Tremendous" Jones

good dose of re-organization in order to feel the
passion again.

The issues of life are dynamic. You are aiming
at moving targets and running races with no clear
finishing line. You have responsibilities, energy levels,
health factors, relationship variances, and expectation
shortfalls to deal with. It's no wonder your passion
goes AWOL from time to time. Often, it gets pushed
out the door by other forces.

If our passion has gone missing, then it's a
matter of life management, not trading our life in on
a new one! As Charlie "Tremendous" Jones would
say, "If you want to be successful, don't look for
something better, become better at what you do and
success will find you." Becoming better at what you
do sometimes calls for you to rearrange the furniture
of your life.

Many of the factors that can drain our passion are noble factors—from transporting our kids to soccer to building our businesses. They are important parts of our lives, but if they suck us dry, they have over-stepped their boundaries. Be proficient in organizing life components so that you can maintain your passion for the kid's soccer and building your business. If you don't manage life, you will be managed by the whims of your circumstances. Circumstances won't leave any room at the inn for passion unless you make room for it. Create space for your passion to breath and passion will spur you on to succeed.

Associate with passionate people

When we feel like our fire has gone out, being around the right people can ignite our flagging spirit. In the words of Albert Schweitzer, "In everyone's life, at some time, our inner fire goes out. It is then burst into flame by an encounter with another human being. We should all be thankful for those people who rekindle the inner spirit."

> If you want more passion in your life, hang around passionate people.

The passions of passionate people rub off on us. A football coach once said to one of his players, "You're doing well, young man. The way you hit the lines, and the way you dodge, tackle and dive is marvelous." The player responded, "It comes easy to me coach—I used to go shopping with my mother!"

If you want more passion in your life, hang around passionate people. Our temperaments subconsciously start to mimic the temperaments of the people with whom we keep company. As Warren Buffett says, "Pick out associates whose behavior is better than yours and you will drift in that direction."

It works the other way as well. Be careful about the company that you keep. The wrong people can be the biggest passion drainers of all. If you are lacking passion, do an assessment of the people with whom you are spending most your time. You may be lacking passion because your relational environment has little or no inspirational value.

Hang out with passionate motivated people. When you do, make sure that you're not a drain on them, otherwise you won't be invited back! Don't forget that there is nothing to stop you from being an initiator of passionate people getting together. Be someone who not only adds passion to an environment, but also be one who initiates the gathering of passionate people.

Dream to change the world

Being a dreamer is more than just imagining you and your loved ones laying out on a beach in Tahiti. Yes, relaxing on an exotic beach is a great dream, but you should dream to change the world as well. In fact, you have a responsibility to dream for the benefit of mankind. Humanity depends on dreamers. Stop to think how many innovations have made our lives better. The microwave oven, cell phones, plane travel, the internet, antibiotics and lest we forget the person who discovered anesthetic!

These were all just dreams in the minds of their inventors. These inventors were fueled by a dream to solve a problem or improve life. It motivated them to give everything they had to deliver a solution to mankind.

In the late 1700's, the Yellow Fever virus plagued the United States. People were dying by the thousands and it was devastating the populations of port cities on the East Coast and Gulf states of America. The city of Philadelphia lost ten percent of its population to the deadly virus. Doctors were perplexed as to what was causing it to spread. None of the usual medical defenses, such as modifying human habits, disinfecting homes with vinegar and camphor or the avoidance of sick victims proved effective.

After conscientious research, Cuban physician Carlos Finlay concluded that the transmission of the virus was not directly from human to human but involved an intermediary. In this case, it was the mosquito. But his odd theory that the mosquito was responsible for the spread of the killer disease was ridiculed for years. *The Washington Post* called Finlay's mosquito theory "silly and nonsensical." All the while, Yellow Fever was inflicting its deadly toll. The French abandoned their attempt to continue building the Panama Canal due to, in no small part, thousands of workers dying from Yellow Fever.

> The Washington Post called Finlay's mosquito theory "silly and nonsensical."

After twenty fruitless years of working tirelessly to gain scientific acceptance of his theory, Carlos Finlay's work was eventually picked up by physicians Walter Reed, Jesse Lazear and William Gorgas. These physicians dedicated their lives to the dream of eradicating the virus that was killing family members by the thousands. Jesse Lazear died as a result of being infected during one of his clinical trials. But their dreams were finally realized. They cracked the code to conquering the virus and stopped the carnage to human life. By applying the methods first recommended by Finlay, Yellow Fever was controlled to such an extent that the construction work on the Panama Canal was completed.

The plague was not eradicated by itself. It took many people with a dream to find a solution to a lethal problem for it to happen. The fulfillment of their dream changed the world. Today, there are still biotechnologists around the world who painstakingly work around the clock with the dream to solve more of the countless medical riddles of the human body.

Every one of us has the capacity to leave the world a better place for us having lived here. Problems abound and improvements are needed. The world is in need of people who dream of being the solution. Don't be a lazy dreamer, or a selfish one. Don't spend your life enjoying the benefits of someone else's achieved dreams and not seek to improve the world for those that follow us. Become impassioned by having a dream that leads to improvement in the lives of others. There's nothing wrong with dreaming of a nice home and traveling the world but don't stop there. Dream a dream that helps your fellow man and you will unleash a passion within you that is potent and world changing.

Stoke up the love factor

The fires of passion are ignited by the sparks of love. Often the cause of our numbness and lack of passion is that our love has lost its spark. While this can apply to romance and lovers, I am speaking in far greater terms. Love is a decision we make, not an emotion we feel.

We have a capacity to love people, even when they least deserve it; even when there is no reciprocation. We are simply that capable—capable of loving others, just because we choose to love them. We are at our best when we love. The more we love, the better we become. The more we love, the more passion we have for life and the better we feel about our future. As Franklin P. Jones said, "Love doesn't make the world go 'round.' Love is what makes the ride worthwhile."

I have discovered in my life that being self-absorbed eventually undermines my level of passion for life. I realize that "me" is just not enough reason to keep myself fired up. On the other hand, nothing makes me come alive more than when I have self-lessly cared for others. In times when we are lacking passion, this might be a worthwhile question to ask of ourselves, "Have I been thinking too much about myself and my needs?"

Now, I understand the value of loving our-selves, but if that's all we do, there's a high chance our preoccupation with self will cause our passion level to wane. There is something about loving others that fires up our spirit and joy for living. So if your passion lacks heat, it could be that your love has grown cold. It happens all the time. Sometimes we become so busy with responsibilities that we forget that our greatest impact in this world comes from how we love, not in what we achieve. Having said that, I think there is a strong case for saying, the more we love, the more we will achieve.

Keep your focus looking ahead

Looking too intently upon your past can drain your passion for the present as well as the future. Everyone botches things up in their life. There's not a person on the planet who doesn't wish they could go back and change some things in their past. But the starting point for "do-overs" is always right now and not some time in the past!

Regarding the direction that we focus, people seem to fall into two groups—those who keep looking back and trying to make sense of the broken or missing pieces and those who move forward giving their mental energy to the future. A friend of mine says, "You won't know where you're heading if you are always looking back." How true that is. We wouldn't dream of driving a car forward while only looking in the rearview mirror. Yet, how many times do we crash the opportunities of our future because we try to move ahead with our eyes fixed on what's behind. I am not saying that it's not important to occasionally reference the past so that you don't make the same mistake twice. But never let an occasional reference lure you into holding a lingering gaze.

Ruminating over the unchangeable past is not a good recipe for mental health! In motor vehicles, there is a reason that the rearview mirror is small and the windshield large. You're meant to spend most of your time looking to where you're heading and only an occasional glance to your past. It's our hopes and dreams for the future, not our history, that stirs up our passion. Keep your focus looking ahead. Stay loyal to your vision and it will fuel your passion.

Use your insecurity to your advantage

One of the fascinating things about humanity is that we are insecure. There is not a person on the planet who isn't insecure and with a deep desire to be accepted. From the person wanting to fit into a certain size of clothing to the person wanting to drive a certain style of vehicle, the whole human race is striving for approval to some degree. I have spent time with famous people, rich people, beautiful people, and successful people all with the attributes that you would think render a person immune to insecurity. But, like everyone, they have their struggles with wanting to be approved by their fellow man. Oh, some may have moments when they come across so self-assured, but don't be bamboozled by them. Sharon Osbourne stated recently, "Fame doesn't insulate you from insecurity. If anything, it magnifies self-doubt."

> Use your insecurity to drive you to become something distinctive.

All the education and counseling in the world has not eradicated the basic propensity of human nature towards insecurity. So use it to your advantage. The need for acceptance can ignite within a person a passion to prove themselves. Use your insecurity to drive you to become something distinctive.

We live in a world where people take notice and make way for those who have proven them- selves in some endeavor. Some people become so irritated with not being noticed that they fire up and prove themselves just for the sake of getting some honor and admiration. Proving yourself will get you noticed. It may also elevate the quality of your life if you can steward the success wisely. What it won't do is eradicate your insecurity. You need something more powerful than your achievements and the adulation of others to do that. But, proving yourself to others can still fire you up with the determination to improve your life in some aspects. Whether it's a credible method for attaining mental peace is open for debate. But there's no denying it, a desire to prove yourself to others can release passion in you to improve the world and your position in it.

Recall your calling

There is an element of mystery about this passion inducer. Not everyone experiences this, but some do and it is a very powerful motivator. At an epiphany point in their journey, some people sense a mysterious calling to do something specific with their lives. They experience what some liken to a divine communiqué. Recently, a major league baseball player turned his back on a multi-million dollar pro- fessional baseball salary to join the priesthood. He left a life that comes with lots of wine, women, and money and has committed to a life of just a little wine, no money or women. What motivates a man to make such a decision? A calling—a passion for something greater than fame and fortune.

The "calling" is not just limited to entering the priesthood. Paul J. Meyer, a world renowned businessman and philanthropist, sensed a calling upon his life to make money so that he could generously support charitable causes. To this end, he gave away over sixty million dollars before he passed away in 2009. Giving money was his calling and so that made Paul J. Meyer very passionate about making as much as he could.

For those of you who have experienced that mysterious calling upon your life, reconnecting with that calling will re-energize your passion for what you were called to do.

Bounce off rock bottom

There is a type of passion that comes from hitting rock bottom. When you get so sick and tired of living an unsatisfying life, a passion can explode within you to finally do something about it. Jim Rohn said it this way, "I have discovered that 'things' never change—not by themselves. It's when a human, with sufficient disgust, desire, and determination to change his life finally shouts, 'I have had it with defeat and humiliation, and I will tolerate it no longer.'" Let me share with you one such occurrence in my life.

For many years of my adult life, I had rationalized away being overweight. I drew upon great medical myths like, "I have big bone structure" as an explanation for my weighing at least thirty percent more than I should. I considered myself being "a

little overweight," but never admitted to being signif-
icantly so. I knew that I could fit into jeans with a
certain waist size and only when I found myself
having to buy jeans the next size up, would I be
willing to admit that I had crept over a line. If I had a
photo shoot lined up, I would throw myself into *The
Cabbage Soup Diet* for a few weeks prior to the shoot.
The diet along with some limited camera angles and
strategic lighting would eliminate my double chin,
but barely so. There is only so much digital photo
correction one can do to erase the signs of calorie
overdosing.

I have appreciated living in a fashion era
whereby guys wear shirts un-tucked. This helped to
hide the evidence. But I hated going shopping for
new jeans because my love for
high-glycemic carbohydrates such
as bread, fries, pasta and sweets,
would be found out. When I was
younger, if my weight crept beyond
a certain range, I could hit the gym
for a few weeks and pare the
weight down. But with every pass-
ing year, the quick fixes of intensive

> When you get so sick
> and tired of living an
> unsatisfying life a
> passion can explode
> within you to finally
> do something about it.

workouts, running, and cabbage soup diets were less
effective. The weight became harder to eliminate. All
the while, my fat cells expanded little by little every
time I comforted and entertained myself with food.
Then the day came when the weight of all those little
excesses caused my rationalizations to collapse.

In preparation for a special event, I put on
my favorite suit. It was the classiest suit I had ever
owned. I bought it from an exclusive men's store in

Melbourne, Australia. But as I squeezed myself into it, the exquisite lines of the suit were lost. Instead of the suit making me look great, I made the suit look cheap. As I stood in front of the full length mirror, a tidal wave of reality hit me. In that moment, the thought that I was just "a little overweight" was laid bare as a case of denial. The thought that I could get back into an "acceptable weight range" with a round of cabbage soup and a few weeks at the gym was delusional. Trimming down was not going to take weeks, but probably six months or more. There was no legitimate reason for me to be in that shape. I was to blame. Without concern for my health, I had eaten myself into a hole and hit rock bottom.

I set up my camera and tripod and took a series of unflattering photographs to document my physique. The photos were embarrassing. Without doubt, the excess weight was placing undue stress upon my heart and had given my feet a painful case of plantar fasciitis. Looking at the photographs fueled a desire to change for the better. Hitting rock bottom created a passion to improve. It had been ages since I felt good about my health and how my clothes fit. I became passionate to create a new reality. Sometimes you have to hit bottom to bounce back up.

Beat others up the ladder

If the ladder is leaning up against the right wall, then beat others to the top. We are by nature born with a competitive spirit. Use it to your advantage! One of the reasons why I like to associate with successful people is that it gooses my competitive spirit. It especially brings my passion to a boil and motivates me to lift my game when I see people who are younger than me doing better than me!

There are times when my passion stems from a pure spirit of wanting to benefit my fellow man. There are other times where my passion comes from a desire to *beat* my fellow man! I suppose there should be a balance between the two. Don't buy

> If someone is winning more awards than you, don't get jealous and frustrated. Get motivated and beat them!

into the philosophy that "life's not a competition" as a means to justify sitting on the sidelines. Competition can be healthy and we should use it to spur each other on to greater effectiveness. If someone is winning more awards than you, don't get jealous and frustrated. Get motivated and beat them!

Throw down the gauntlet

In days of old, when one knight wanted to challenge another knight to a duel, he would remove his protective glove, called a gauntlet, and throw it on the ground in front of his opponent. If the opponent picked up the glove, it was a sign to the challenger that the duel was accepted. Hence we get the term, "throwing down the gauntlet."

Issuing a challenge has a long history. It appeals to something within us to want to rise to the challenge. Often people's passions are unleashed when they are given a personal challenge. Any team leader needs to become adept at "gauntlet throwing." That means taking off the protective glove, thereby making yourself a little vulnerable and throwing down the challenge to your team.

There is an art to issuing a challenge. You can use the reward challenge. For example, "I challenge you to achieve this level and if you do, you will be rewarded with a trip to Hawaii." Or the less altruistic threat gauntlet can be used. For example, "Achieve this level or you will need to find yourself a new team."

Sometimes leaders bravely use the element of humiliation as a challenge technique. For example saying to someone in front of their team mates, "I don't think you're capable of doing this. You haven't got what it takes!" The team member feels so humiliated by what the leader says that they pick up the glove and succeed just to spite the leader! Of course the leader knows all along that they were capable, but they just used this technique to light a fire under their team member. While this can be a very effective form of throwing down the challenge, be careful because it can backfire. On one occasion I used this technique and not only did the person not rise to the challenge, they never talked to me again!

> Any team leader needs to become adept at "gauntlet throwing."

On the whole, people like to be challenged—especially when there is a reward involved. People love to be affirmed by their team members when they succeed in meeting a challenge. It is often what is needed to stir the passions of people into action.

Can you throw down the gauntlet on yourself?

Not effectively. We can make bold statements to ourselves and when it gets tough, we just as easily talk ourselves out of our commitments. But it can be effective if you enlist the support of a fellow team member. You can make a pact to challenge each other and keep each other accountable. In effect, throw the gauntlet down on each other. It is human nature to rise to a challenge especially when there is a desirable reward involved. Take advantage of this human propensity to fire up your passion to succeed.

Choose to be passionate

Ultimately, passion is a choice. The difference between the motivated and the apathetic often comes down to this. Motivated people train themselves to be passionate. Apathetic people wait to feel inspired by someone else or wait until the circumstances are conducive to being passionate.

You may ask, "What about finding a vocation that I love so much that mustering passion is never a problem?" Admittedly that sounds good and the "do what you love and the money will follow" philosophy is popular. But I find that notion can set people up for a life of constantly being restless—always searching for that "ideal" something. My experience has taught me that the big rewards follow people who choose to enthusiastically do what other people are reluctant to do. Teaching yourself to be passionate about doing hard things provides the best payoff.

Too many people spend their whole lives jumping around from one opportunity to another and going broke in the process. They're searching for something that requires no mustering of passion because the passion just "naturally flows." It is commendable to move in the direction of your passions. It certainly makes better sense to derive an income from doing something that you love doing. But I also know that if you can't get your passion to pay your bills, then anxiety and worry will erode your zest.

On the other hand, far more people have succeeded in life because they committed themselves to a viable venture and have chosen to be passionate about it—even when they didn't feel like it. Get as close as you can to your passion, but realize there are components of every income producing endeavor that won't thrill you. Learn to be passionate by choice and you will save yourself from wasting a lot of time and money from jumping around with EADD (enterprise attention deficit disorder)!

> Big rewards follow people who choose to enthusiastically do what other people are reluctant to do.

Now to the How to: Passion

1. Purposely create an opportunity for you to increase your passion. Rearrange something in your life to give you the time to reconnect with your passion.

2. Reclassify yourself as a passionate person by nature. Do not depend on right circumstances to become passionate. Be passionate by decision.

3. Take someone who has the quality of passion out to lunch. Yes, you pay! Determine where their passion comes from and incorporate those qualities into your life.

4. Expand your dream so that it benefits your wider community—the world!

5. Regularly meet with other passionate people. Create the opportunity if such an environment does not exist.

Quick FUEL: Passion

There is no passion to be found playing small—in settling for a life that is less than the one you are capable of living. *Nelson Mandela*

Our passions are the winds that propel our vessel. Our reason is the pilot that steers her. Without winds the vessel would not move and without a pilot she would be lost. *Proverb*

The most powerful weapon on earth is the human soul on fire. *Field Marshal Ferdinand Foch*

Most people are underpowered than overworked. *Anon*

A great leader's courage to fulfill his vision comes from passion, not position. *John Maxwell*

Nothing great in the world has been accomplished without passion. *Georg Wilhelm Friedrich Hegel*

Those endowed with passion may perform very good or very bad acts. All depends on the principles which direct them. *Napoleon Bonaparte*

Passions make men live, knowledge merely makes them last. *Chamfort*

We must act out passion before we can feel it. *Jean-Paul Sartre*

There is no greatness without a passion to be great, whether it's the aspiration of an athlete or an artist, a scientist, a parent, or a businessperson. *Anthony Robbins*

I believe that education is all about being excited about something. Seeing passion and enthusiasm helps push an educational message. *Steve Irwin*

Success Workshop: Passion

1. Are you a naturally passionate person or do you need to constantly choose to be passionate? Rate yourself on the following scale.

Passionate by choice   Passionate by nature

2. Name two things in your life that currently drain you and leave you feeling passionless about your life:

_____

_____

What could you rearrange in your life to create more room for passion?

_____

_____

_____

3. Name three people who you admire for being passionate in what they do:

_____

_____

_____

What are the characteristics of their passion that impress you?

_____

_____

_____

_____

Which of the above characteristics could you start imitating today?

_____

4. Name three situations where you can display more passion:

_____

_____

_____

5. Risk

The desire for safety stands against
every noble human endeavor.
Tacitus

Four high school boys cut classes until after lunch and gave the excuse that they had experienced a flat tire on the way to school. "Well," said the teacher, "You will have to make up the test that you missed this morning." Placing them in the four corners of the room so they could not see each other's answers, he read the first question: "Which tire was flat?"

Some risks are not worth the risk. But while some risks are not worth taking, ultimately there is no way to succeed while always playing it safe. Entrepreneurs of all types attribute their success to a willingness to take risks—courses of action for which no one guarantees a favorable outcome.

It's understandable why there is a natural aversion to taking a risk. Basically, we want to avoid suffering, sorrow and embarrassment. Our natural logic leads us to think that if it doesn't work out according to our plans, then we will be left worse off than before taking the leap. Such a conclusion is not unwarranted. The advice "don't bet the farm" is there because people, in their pursuit of something better, have been known to lose so much when reality fell short of expectation. Yet, to live safely within one's comfort zone can be the most dangerous place of all. You can lose so much more by always playing it safe. If you don't risk failure, you risk never knowing success. Trying to secure your safety by never venturing out of the comfort zone is to inflict possibly the greatest harm upon your life. As Goethe said, "The dangers of life are infinite, and among them is safety."

> Taking risks won't guarantee success but not taking risks will guarantee your smallest life possible.

The fear of failure or the regret of missed opportunities equally imprisons the spirit of a person. The only way out is by taking risks. Albeit, taking risks won't guarantee success, but not taking risks will ensure living your smallest life possible. In the long run, the cost of a small life will be far more expensive than any losses incurred while pursuing a great life. The price of a life without risk demands the sacrifice of every success a person could have otherwise enjoyed. Throw that in with the ache of lamenting "what could have been," and the cost of a safe life is expensive. At all costs, avoid a life where you take no risks.

Get over the fear of being embarrassed

Whatever happened to us in the playgrounds of our youth sure had an impact on our fragile self esteems. We hate to be laughed at and abhor being the object of ridicule. How much of who we are as adults has been molded around the psychological bullying and teasing we received as kids? I suspect a lot. Nevertheless, while the source of ridicule may be different for all of us, it has had the same deprecating effects on us. I think author Mignon McLaughlin summed it up best when he wrote, "The fear of being laughed at makes cowards of us all." Someone else expanded on that by saying, "Many great ideas have been lost because the people who had them could not stand being laughed at."

In my experience, the only way to overcome the fear of embarrassment is to have lots of embarrassments. It cures you. Eventually you realize that the only way to die from embarrassment is to do so by your own hands. In some countries, they mandate for all their citizens two years of national service in their nation's military. I think a good idea would be for every young person to spend two years as politicians. More than any other position in a free democracy, politicians get criticized, ridiculed and scorned. Sometimes I wonder how politicians handle all the negative attacks. But they do. They just get used to it. They toughen up. No one is born naturally tough. You become that way by surviving lots of abrasions.

> No one is born naturally tough. You become that way by surviving lots of abrasions.

If you want to succeed, shake off your fear of ridicule, scorn or laughter. Avoiding ridicule doesn't make you secure, it keeps you vulnerable. The fear of being laughed at will keep you timid and broke.

Learn to laugh at yourself first, then you are always ahead of those who would laugh at you. That is a key to diffusing the effect of embarrassment. See yourself as the initiator of fun even when the fun is at your expense. Embarrassment is a manifestation of either pride or insecurity. Both are dangerous elements to have in your temperament if you are trying to engage people. Be the first to acknowledge your quirks to others, so when you do something that attracts some laughter, you can laugh right along with them. Everyone has a good time and you have effectively conquered pride and insecurity with every chuckle. Get over your fear of being embarrassed.

Get over the fear of losing it all

You would think that those who have lost it all would be the ones who most fear losing it all. That's not the case. People who have been through the unfortunate experience of being wiped out realize that life still goes on and that you do recover. Often, you don't discover your own resilience and strength until you do face being wiped out.

Robert H. Schuller tells the story of his boyhood when a tornado completely destroyed their family home and farm. Nothing was left, not even rubble. The tornado was like a giant vacuum that sucked up everything, leaving nothing but a clean cement foundation. With a young family depending on him, Schuller's dad took a claw hammer and started pulling bent nails from pieces of old lumber. Schuller tells of how he watched his dad straighten out those nails and use them to rebuild their lives.

We fear that losing it all will be the death of us. On the contrary, so many who have brilliantly succeeded did so because they first lost it all. Many of those who have to start all over again, gather it back in half the time than it took to gather it in the first place. The wisdom gained in the journey gives them tremendous traction the second time around.

There could even be a case for the benefit of losing it all at least once in your life. It helps you realize just how capable you are of surviving and rebuilding. Now can you go overboard in risking too much? Yes. Especially if you have a family depending upon you to put food on the table, you better not be a gambling fool. While taking risks is essential to succeeding, "betting the farm" is a bad approach.

> A lot of great empires have been built with straightened nails.

Years ago a business entrepreneur, whose extraordinary financial success was gained against the backdrop of a painful bankruptcy, gave me this advice, "Build your castle, put a moat around it, then go for it knowing that you always have a home to which you can return, win or lose." In effect, he was saying take bold risks but don't risk so much that you put your family's safety and basic provisions in jeopardy. There's a saying, "Go big or go home!" It sounds brazen and courageous, but to that I would add, "Don't go so big that if it doesn't work out, your family has no home to go home to!"

Danger lies in the extremes of either not risking at all or risking too much. Some people err on the side of playing it too safe for fear of losing it all. Others, like Icarus in Greek mythology, try to fly to the sun on wings of wax and feathers. They are always risking it all on the "big one" that will solve all of their problems. Invariably, they come crashing back to earth. For those of you who are ardent risk takers, remember that intelligent risks are totally different from wishful gambles. For those of you who are risk resistant because you fear losing it all, know that losing it all will not be the death of you. A lot of great empires have been built with straightened nails.

Get over the need for guarantees

Have you ever heard of the term "the guarantee of faith?" No. They call it the "leap of faith" for a reason. That is because there is no guarantee as to exactly how you're going to land. Many people aren't willing to take a risk because they're not sure how it's all going to work out. To advance you must become accustomed to taking risks without the benefit of any guarantees. As former footballer Jim McMahon said, "Yes, risk taking is inherently failure-prone. Otherwise, it would be called sure-thing-taking."

The world of business is largely based on this caveat: Past results are no guarantee of future performance. Free enterprise is a faith game—faith that the wise application of business principles, procedures and persistence will lead to more success than failure. But at the end of the day, no one gives absolute assurance to the outcomes. The only guarantee is that you can't succeed without taking risks.

Get over the past bad experience

Who wants to, after having been burned, go in for a second helping? Who in their right mind would want to try again when the first attempt capsized?

Let me start by saying that when you have put much on the line, it is acutely painful to fail. I don't want to minimize it. There's nothing I could say to put any real glamour into failure. It just stinks when something which you have put so much hope into, only succeeds in making you feel terrible. To dream of sweet success and instead be handed a whopping failure is brutal on your self esteem. Regaining your confidence and trusting your instincts again can take a while. Even the finest of chocolate has its limits on what it can do to heal the hurting spirit!

If your last experience was a disaster, it is vital to follow it up with a good experience to stop the bad one from secreting its degrading poison into how you perceive yourself. Failure may deepen your character but it comes dangerously close to defining your character if you simmer in its juices too long. It is imperative to stop a past bad experience from having the upper hand in defining who you are.

> "Life is too short and I don't want to waste a second of it by holding on to hurts or disappointments."
> Chris Falson

If a failure makes you resist ever taking another risk, you have elevated that failure to the governorship of your life. Never let one specific episode have that much power over you. Keep taking risks and even if you experience a plethora of failures, you have saved yourself from being defined by a particular one. The essential key is not to back away from taking further risks but to put into practice what you learn each time something doesn't work out. Application of what you learn is preparation for eventual success.

Co-founder of *People of the Second Chance*, Mike Foster, sums it up best:

"When you experience a personal tragedy your natural human response is to 'protect yourself.' Not wanting to ever go through that pain again, every thought, action, decision and relationship is run through the filter of that tragedy. It makes logical sense to protect yourself—hold back something in relationships. To hedge. Minimize risk. To dream smaller.

Ironically though, it isn't the unfortunate experience that ruins your life. It is the protective mode you put in place to deal with your wounds. You stop living. You became a hostage to your hurt, instead of learning from it. Life becomes a cheap version of what you are truly created for. It is a choice in how we respond to these situations. We can close up and shut down or we can learn and then trust again."

The world is always in need of people who succeed as a result of learning from past efforts that didn't succeed. It is the person who rises from the pile of failures who relates most profoundly in helping others to do the same. Keep taking risks.

Become an intelligent risk taker

Taking a risk and taking a gamble are two very different things. Gambling is putting your welfare in the hands of nothing more substantive than rolling the dice and hoping for the best. If you are taking action based on very little hard evidence or vastly incomplete data, you're probably gambling.

During the years of what we now call "the technology bubble," Warren Buffett was mocked for not investing in technology stocks. His response was simple, "I don't invest in things I don't understand." When the entire tech sector melted down a few years later, Buffett avoided the bloodbath. He was a genius again! If opportunities are presented that involve highly sophisticated and complex details, Buffett avoids them. He considers investing in things he doesn't understand to be, for him, simply gambling.

A maxim of life is that understanding breeds tolerance. Your tolerance for risk should come from understanding the upside, downside, inside and out-side of what is involved. Blind ignorance and hopeful sentiments should not be the basis for taking a risk. When speaking of risks that end up hurting you, investment expert, Burt White, puts a lot of blame at the feet of over-ambitious as-sumptions, lack of risk controls, and poor contingency planning. Often "the risk" gets the blame

> "The road of life is full of potholes. Any plan that requires dodging them all is a plan for disaster."
> Warren Buffett

when things go south. Whereas the real cause of misfortune was not the risk but the lack of patience and due diligence that would have made taking the risk ill-advised in the first place.

As the chief architect of your future, you need to be the risk initiator. But don't be bullied into taking a risk that you don't understand. Don't risk without wise counsel and a full reckoning of the possible costs involved. Success never unfolds in a straight line. So your risk taking must accommodate the inevitability of some things not performing as well as you hoped. As Buffett says, "The road of life is full of potholes. Any plan that requires dodging them all is a plan for disaster." Take into account that things do go wrong, but don't let the possibility of something going wrong stop you from ever taking a risk. Take risks but make them intelligent ones.

Whether rolling the dice with your last dollar or playing it safe, both are a gamble that puts too much hope in chance outcomes. Intelligent risk taking is never a gamble. While there is never a guarantee of outcomes, experienced risk takers always check for submerged rocks before they dive in. They know that "hoping for the best" is not a strategy for success. They also know that never diving in will ruin the prospects for ultimately achieving great things. Be an intelligent risk taker and increase your risk taking! The world has many effective risk takers and you are joining them.

Grow faster

You will grow faster in a shorter amount of time by taking risks. Do everything you can to avoid making mistakes, but remember that being scared of making mistakes is the biggest mistake of all. If you are languishing without much progress, do a personal risk assessment. Recently a friend asked me, "What have you planned for this year that you would consider to be dangerous?" It stumped me for a moment. He wasn't advocating for me take up base jumping but he did effectively highlight a hole in my plans.

While I had prepared a long list of formidable quests for the year, I could categorize them as hard, but not dangerous. While they would call for great effort, I was not putting much on the line besides exertion. My friend challenged me to include something in my year that put me in danger of having the walls of my comfort zone blown out. Settling into a slow pace of personal growth is not my idea of abundant living. Neither should it be yours. What in your plans would you consider dangerous?

Increase your connectability

People connect more with your failures than your successes. While they may admire your achievements, they will relate more to your challenges. It's the story of overcoming your difficulties that gives people hope that they can do the same. What George Torok said is so true, "We admire

> Being risk adverse makes you socially boring. It's the thrills and the spills of our lives that make us interesting to others.

most those who can make a comeback—who can get up from a stumble. We admire that more than one who has had a smooth sailing."

One of the dangers in being risk adverse is that you minimize your capacity to relate to others. If you have never risked and lost, then your ability to connect with the hearts of others is limited. It's through your dramas that people most strongly identify with you—the risks that you took, the ones that failed, and how you kept going. People are inspired by stories.

Don't risk having a low identity factor with others. Lean towards taking as many risks as you can bear. You will be rewarded with an increased relevancy factor to other people of like pursuit. Being risk adverse makes you, plain and simple, socially boring. It's the thrills and the spills of our lives that make us interesting. If you shelter yourself from the potential of failure or discomfort, you'll have no inspiring experiences to share. So get out there and take some risks so that you can bring an interesting life to the success party.

Increase your independence

Being adverse to risk not only ensures the absence of the success, but it ushers in the presence of dependency. As every farmer knows, planting in the spring supplants the need for welfare in the fall. Not taking the risk to produce something valuable to others is to risk becoming dependent upon the kindness of others. Don't be dependent upon the harvest gained from other people's risk taking. Be the one who takes the risks and is rewarded with independence and freedom.

Increase your boldness

How high can you go? You will rise until you hit the ceiling of your timidity. Some people's timidity holds them down so much that they can hardly raise their voice. One day, I stopped at a café and put in my order. As I stood near the counter waiting for my meal, one of the young cashiers was trying to get the attention of a man who had ordered a slice of cheesecake. He was standing over to the side and not paying attention. Her first few attempts of saying, "Sir, your cheesecake is ready," landed on deaf ears.

It was a noisy lunchtime crowd and the cashier was speaking so timidly that he couldn't hear her. I watched her try a few more times. With every attempt to get his attention, she became increasingly self-conscious and exasperated. It got to the point where I was tempted to say, "Listen sweetheart, the man saw the picture of the cheesecake on the menu, he ordered it, he paid for it, he's probably salivating like Pavlov's dogs to bite into it. For goodness sake, SPEAK UP and let the man know his cheesecake is ready!"

You can't be timid if you want to advance in this world. Take the risk, be bold, especially if you have a product or service that can help people.

Now to the How to: Risk

1. Eliminate the erroneous mindset that security comes with not taking risks.

2. Evaluate your current action plan and determine whether it has any trends toward or away from taking risks.

3. Meet with a mentor for the purpose of evaluating your historical risk tolerance.

4. Establish a risk "no-fly zone." Those things that are too valuable to risk losing such as your family home, or your relational fidelity etc.

5. Start a risk ledger. Draw a line down the middle of a page. On the right side of the page, list the risks that proved worthwhile and on the left side, list the risks that didn't turn out well. Be motivated by the right side and draw out the lessons from the left side.

6. Make the subject of taking risks the focus of your next team meeting. Challenge people to sign up to do something that's going to mean risking something.

Quick FUEL: Risk

Security is mostly a superstition. It does not exist in nature, nor do the children of men as a whole experience it. Avoiding danger is no safer in the long run than outright exposure. Life is either a daring adventure or nothing. *Helen Keller*

A ship in harbor is safe—but that is not what ships are built for. *John A. Shedd*

Often the difference between a successful person and a failure is not one has better abilities or ideas, but the courage that one has to bet on one's ideas, to take a calculated risk and to act. *Andre Malraux*

A man would do nothing if he waited until he could do it so well that no one would find fault with what he has done. *Cardinal Newman*

Of all the people I have ever known, those who have pursued their dreams and failed have lived a much more fulfilling life than those who have put their dreams on a shelf for fear of failure. *Anon*

Progress always involves risk; you can't steal second base and keep your foot on first.
Frederick Wilcox

Take calculated risks. That is quite different from being rash. *General George S. Patton*

Most people can do extraordinary things if they have the confidence or take the risks. Yet most people don't. They sit in front of the TV and treat life as if it goes on forever. *Philip Andrew Adams*

If you're not making mistakes, you're not taking risks, and that means you're not going anywhere. The key is to make mistakes faster than the competition, so you have more chances to learn and win.
John W. Holt, Jr.

People who don't take risks generally make about two big mistakes a year. People who do take risks generally make about two big mistakes a year.
Peter F. Drucker

Success Workshop: Risk

1. Are you a natural risk taker or are you more prone to be cautious? Rate yourself on the following scale.

Cautious   Adventurous

2. Who do you know that takes big risks?

_____

What can you note (positive or negative) about their experience?

_____

_____

_____

3. What is the riskiest thing you have ever done?

_____

_____

How did it turn out?

_____

_____

4. What are three areas in your life that could bene-fit from you being willing to risk more?

_____

_____

_____

5. What one thing could you do this week that is dangerous to your comfort zone?

_____

_____

6. Skill

What a profoundly satisfying feeling when one
finally gets on top of a new set of skills and
then sees the light under the new door
those skills can open.
Gail Sheehy

I wish that all you needed in life was a good attitude in order to succeed. But there are a lot of ingredients to the success recipe and skill happens to be one of them. Abraham Lincoln memorably said that if he had eight hours to cut down a tree, he would spend the first six hours sharpening his axe. A blunt axe in the hands of an optimist is going to do a better job at felling the optimist rather than the tree. A good attitude, in combination with good skills, is a formidable partnership. If you build your skills at the same time as honing your attitudes, the resulting success of that partnership will be a constant fuel source to you and your team.

People Skills

As Theodore Roosevelt said, "The most important single ingredient in the formula of success is knowing how to get along with people." Of all the books written on this subject, I know of none as potent as Dale Carnegie's *How to Win Friends and Influence People.* His book will help you master the basics of positively interacting with people.

One major way to upsurge your people skills is to move outside of your natural sociological parameters. Sociologists say that people tend to effectively communicate with people fifteen years either side of their age. So if you are forty-two years of age, you will relate to people up to age fifty-seven on the high side and twenty-seven years of age on the low side. But that doesn't have

> Opportunities come through new connections more than old, tired connections.

to be the case. Refuse to let that be said about you. You are never mandated to connect only with a certain age range. Love and effort transcends all sociological boundaries. You connect with people by participating in and being interested in their world. As you do, your people skills flourish even more.

Increasing your connections is the key to new motivation for you. The spectrum of humanity is vast. Don't limit yourself to people within your age range or your cultural group. When you experience for the first time whole-hearted connection with an entirely different people group than what you are used to, it releases new passion within you. Don't ever allow yourself to be limited by traditional mindsets and cultural barriers. You are as relevant to people as you decide to be.

I delighted in hearing Charlie "Tremendous" Jones speaking to an audience of young people. He would enthusiastically say to them, "I love speaking to teenagers. Do you know why? Because I have been a teenager for sixty-three years!" Charlie loved people of all ages and was prepared to talk to people of any age. Charlie was a good connector with any age group because he was always prepared with a few jokes and stories that related to them.

My friend, Mike Darnold, is sixty-six years of age. He seems much younger than that because he spends most his time with young people, helping them to learn life skills. In the spring of each year, Mike invites me to speak at a youth camp that he leads for over two hundred young people. Every type of teenage kid is represented at these camps; bold and timid, successful and struggling, secure and abused. Mike relates to them all and is loved by them all. If wealth were measured in relationships, Mike Darnold would be on the list of *Forbes* magazine's *100 Richest Men*. What is Mike's secret? He connects with these kids through the prism of his own embattled past.

For many years, Mike wrestled with alcohol. Although he hasn't touched a drop in thirty years, he has never forgotten that it almost destroyed him. So Mike has dedicated his life to helping young people avoid the pitfalls that he experienced growing up. Connecting with people outside of his age range was simply a choice made by Mike.

Don't let your insecurities inhibit you from reaching out to others. The answer to many of life's dilemmas will be found through relationships. There are many people out there in the world, of all types and ages, whose lives would become better because you cared to get to know them. Opportunities come through new connections more than old, tired connections. Force yourself to expand your relationships to include people outside of your age range and cultural background. This will amplify the power of your people skills.

Learning Skills

What is said about "knowledge being power" is true. That power can propel you forward and take you beyond the confines of your own experiences and skills. Education is fuel for the successful soul. As William Butler once said, "Education is not the filling of a pail, but the lighting of a fire." So, love education!

Value education so much that you are willing to pay for it. Whoever said, "The only certainty in life is death and taxes," should have also included the cost of education. Yet, some people are quick to decry the costs of attending business conferences and purchasing personal development tools. Have you checked into the sticker price of university tuition lately? Education is not cheap and has never been cheap. It costs both money and time. Entrepreneurs don't escape paying for education. They either pay for training or they

> Education makes locksmiths of us all when it comes to opening the doors to success.

pay the price for their lack of training. If one teaching program can teach you what would take years for you to figure out by yourself, enthusiastically pay for it! Desire to increase your skills and accept that skill education requires some financial investment.

If you want more fuel in your life, be earnestly committed to lifelong learning. After extensive studies on the brain, cognitive psychologist and neuroscientist, Daniel J. Levitin, Ph.D., determined, "The brain is plastic. Right through to the end of life the brain is capable of adapting and changing." Education makes locksmiths of us all when it comes to opening the doors to success.

Sales skills

The very thought of "selling" causes many to bristle. I have heard so many people say, "I could never go into sales, I'm just not the sales-type person." Let me gently correct you by saying everyone is in sales. You can't succeed without having to sell something—at the very least, yourself! When you apply for a promotion, you are selling your virtues to your superiors. When you apply for a position within an organization, you are selling the benefits of your expertise to that organization. Obtaining a money loan requires you to put together a proposal and then sell the merits of that proposal to a loan officer. Even

> There's no such person as a "born salesperson." Sales is a relational art form that has a basic logic to it. Learning it takes away much of the fear.

doctors, dentists and lawyers have to advertise and sell their services.

Don't fear selling. There's no such person as a "born salesperson." Sales is a relational art form that has a basic logic to it. Sales skills are learned. While you might think someone is a born salesperson, the reality is that they make it look natural because they have learned the sales process and use it so much that it becomes second nature. When you learn the process and work the process, you will experience the results that the process will bring you. When you start to experience the fruits of the process, you will learn to appreciate being in sales.

> "Everyone lives by selling something."
>
> Robert Louis Stevenson

Here's a basic seven step process to selling that has been proven over the ages. It's a process that applies to the sales of products, services or business opportunities. By learning it and incorporating the steps into your own personality and style, you will have greater confidence in presenting opportunities.

1) Qualify whether the person that you are talking to has the authority to say "yes" if you were to offer them an opportunity. There's no use spending a great degree of your time and emotional energy sharing an opportunity with someone if they are not allowed to take advantage of it.

2) Establish an emotional bond with the person. People like to buy from people they like. So connect

with people in a meaningful way. It doesn't matter how great your service or product is, people won't participate in it if they don't feel connected with you.

3) Ask questions to identify the person's needs. The old maxim, "telling is not selling" is true. I remember sitting at a table in my favorite coffee and tea store. At the table next to me, a businessman sat down with a prospect. After some brief moments of small talk, the businessman started his presentation about the benefits of his product. He talked, talked and talked. I could tell the prospect was bored after the first thirty minutes but he was too polite to stop the salesman mid-pitch. Little did he know, the salesman was just getting warmed up!

Over two hours later, after patiently listening to the businessman go on and on, the prospect excused himself and left. He couldn't wait to get out of there! I did a quick mental tally and determined that the businessman had spoken for 140 minutes compared to the prospect's 5 minutes of talking. The prospect had shown enormous patience whereas, after an hour of the sales pitch, I wanted to get up and bludgeon the salesman with my teapot! His sales skills were giving selling a bad reputation.

Ask questions! Get your prospects sharing about their life and needs. By asking the right leading questions and listening, you will be better positioned to learn about your prospect's needs and your prospect will be more receptive to your solutions.

4) Share the benefits of your product or service as a solution to your prospect's needs. But let your words

be few. We humans have a propensity to talk a lot when we're nervous. We want to minimize any awkward silences, so we resort to filling the silence with the sound of our voice. Don't do it. The more talking you do, the more your success rate plummets. Once you bring a pot of water to a boil, increasing the heat is not going to do anything except create a lot of useless steam. Always err on the side of saying less than talking too much. Share the benefits and get on with the next step in the process.

5) Answer any questions or concerns. Answer only their questions. Don't use this time to answer a whole lot of questions that they have not asked. Keep a rein on how much talking you do.

6) Edify the prospect's authority to make a decision to act. Everyone likes to feel important and respected.

7) Provide a way for the prospect to take immediate action. This is traditionally called "closing the sale." Don't try to convince them with extra words about the benefits of the opportunity. If the prospect is uncertain, revisit step 5 and ask them what their concerns are. Once you have answered their questions, proceed again to steps 6 and 7.

If your prospect is still resistant to taking action, don't push. Harassing somebody into a sale introduces desperation into the mix and everyone's dignity is a casualty. It's better to give a prospect more time to consider the opportunity and have the chance for a follow up than to destroy the relationship by pushing the prospect over the edge.

Here's a summary of my seven step sales process. Photocopy this page and keep it somewhere handy. Whether you use this or develop your own, it's important to have a road map to keep you on course. The more you use it the more natural and effective it will become for you.

Step 1
Qualify whether the person that you are talking to has the authority to say yes.

Step 2
Establish an emotional bond with the person.

Step 3
Ask questions to identify the person's needs.

Step 4
Share the benefits of your product or service as solving your prospect's needs.

Step 5
Ask if they have any questions or concerns.

Step 6
Edify the prospect's authority to make a decision.

Step 7
Provide a way for the prospect to take immediate action.

By having a process to follow when you present opportunities to prospective clients, you will have more confidence. The development of sales skills will fuel better results. Learn this seven step process and use it. You will have to present it several times before it starts to feel natural and uncontrived. Stick with it and you will increase your success rate. Too many people end up blaming their product or service when, in actuality, it's their lack of skill in executing a decent presentation that lets them down.

Gathering skills

Experiencing a meeting with fired up passionate people increases everyone's level of enthusiasm. That's why I am such a proponent of gathering people together—off line! Yes, I appreciate the wonders of the internet and the ability to have webinars and the like, but there is something that stimulates human performance when people physically interact in one room. Electronic interaction cannot emulate the powerful human synergies that result from people and teams physically meeting together.

> If your leader holds events regularly, don't "cherry pick" them by only attending when all the stars line up. Being committed in your attendance is what builds your leadership skills.

People businesses need to provide opportunities for people to physically connect, share their dreams and celebrate their successes. But the event must be well planned, well attended and well programmed. Throwing a meeting together and hoping for the best can backfire!

You are fortunate if you have a leader who hosts events. Plug into them. Volunteer to help. If your leader holds events regularly, don't "cherry pick" them by only attending when all the stars line up. Being committed in your attendance is what builds your leadership skills and favor with your leader.

If you are not connected with a team that already hosts meetings, then start gathering people together. Capitalize on the power that comes from people being with people. But learn the people gathering skills. People won't just show up. When you do get them to show up, they won't come back if they didn't experience value the first time around.

Assembling fifty people in an auditorium that seats five hundred can do more damage than good to establishing an energetic vibe within the group. Giving people a whole row to themselves will only help you if you're an airline! Don't go big with the room and hope that it mysteriously gets filled. That's not big thinking, that's wishful thinking. It's better to book a smaller room and fill it so full that the only way to get in is to come down through the roof! Better to pack out someone's home before you go booking meeting rooms. People gathering in close proximity creates people energy. That's the effect that you want to achieve!

Don't make a few phone calls and put out an email flyer and hope for a good crowd. The name of the game is promote, invite, remind, and get commitments. Keep pumping the event to get the anticipation factor heating up. Unless you are U2, the super rock band, you can't just put on a show and expect people to clamor for a seat.

Packing out a room is still not enough. Don't make the mistake of putting all your effort into getting people there and then provide a half-baked program. It takes a lot of effort to get a good attendance and many a good leader underestimates the drain that this task has on them. I have seen it happen so many times. When it comes to giving an inspiring message at an event, having expended so much emotional and mental energy on the organizational details up to the event, tired leaders deliver random, "off the cuff" thoughts that fail to capitalize on the moment.

If you are taking responsibility for delivering the inspirational goods, then delegate the task of successfully getting a good attendance to someone else. That way you are able to give your energies to the preparation and delivery of an inspiring program that fires up your people. If organizing a well attended event requires too much of your attention, then call in a trusted speaker who can hit a home run for you. Mark Twain once said, "It usually takes me more than three weeks to prepare a good impromptu speech." If you do speak, prepare to be awesome!

> Live inspirational settings give you the competitive edge over the myriad of online community experiences.

When it comes to gathering people effectively, trying to cover all of the major bases yourself will leave you feeling more disappointed than impassioned by the experience. When all is said and done, the person who should be most energized from an event should be the host. If hosting an event almost wipes you out, you won't be inclined to hold another any time soon!

When people gather, it can be a powerhouse of energy but to capitalize on this energy you need to continue the momentum—have one powerful meeting roll into another one coming soon. When people come away having been inspired, they are highly motivated to invite newcomers to the next one. If you wait too long before holding the next meeting because you're burned out, you fail to harness the energy that your initial gathering created.

There are three important components to effectively gathering people:

1) Organizing the right facilities.

2) Getting the people there.

3) Delivering the inspirational goods.

Even when the gathering is smaller in number, one person can't effectively cover all three. So make it a team effort. Getting two out of the three components right is not enough.

Successful meetings and events are extremely effective ways to fuel team spirit. In fact, live inspirational settings give you the competitive edge over the myriad of online community experiences. I relish what the internet can do in bringing people together, but I also know its limitations. People, even if they're introverts, still crave being with other people physically. Hold a great meeting and people will keep coming back to get their passions stirred once again. There's a certain energy that is only released in the context of live human interaction. If your enterprise or organization can facilitate effective "offline" meetings, you will capitalize on what the human spirit longs for and needs—vibrant human interaction.

Leadership skills

In learning to be a leader who dispenses high octane fuel, I have learned that it is not about being dynamic and exciting. It's about building the right things into people. The leader that provides the best fuel to their followers knows the following:

Leadership is about making leaders out of followers.
Being a leader is not about looking good and sounding good and having lots of followers. It's about your ability to build leadership qualities into the lives of your followers. Being a charismatic leader can often get in the way of that happening. I have heard it said that only seven percent of people belong to an organization because of the dynamism of the leader. In fact, studies by top business researchers (such as Jim Collins' book *Good to Great*) have determined that dynamic personalities can be a drawback to growing strength within an organization. The reason is because a strong personality-based leader can take up all the airspace with their brilliance, leaving their followers both mesmerized and frustrated, not to mention, undeveloped.

A mature leader will sacrifice many of their own opportunities to shine for the sake of developing leadership qualities within their followers. It takes heightened understanding for the leader to not let their charismatic qualities be the very thing that stymies the development of their team. I know leaders who have the dynamism of an oat bran muffin and yet they lead a large and loyal team of emerging leaders. It's because they focus on building up the leadership qualities within their team. The substance of a leader is measured by how much they develop leadership qualities within their followers. If you want to build a big team, sacrifice your own opportunities to shine for the sake of the people you're developing.

Truth always stands even if the leader falls short.
There was a time in my life as a leader when my organization was stuck. It had stalled and I just could not get it moving. Everything I tried either failed or returned less than inspiring results. I went to see a friend in a different territory whose organization had taken off with stellar performance. He spent a few hours showing me his growth strategy and then he turned to me and emphatically declared, "Wes, this ain't rocket science!"

So, having heard that I didn't need to be a rocket scientist to succeed, I was pumped. Returning back to my territory, I shared it with my staff and we enacted my friend's strategy exactly as he had recommended. Did it work? Not one bit. Depressed, I determined that if I couldn't make something that wasn't "rocket science" work, I must have been dumb. Or worse yet, dumber than dumb! Eventually, I discovered that strategies are not always transferrable. I learned this by meeting several leaders in my area who had tried the same strategies with the same lousy results.

> Shouting, "This ain't rocket science," or "This is so easy a cave man could do it!" is not being genuine because success doesn't come easily.

Success truths are different from success strategies. Without doubt, strategies are necessary, but I have learned not to overemphasize strategies. Specific tactics can be fallible under the directorship of a different personality. Strategies can fail when relocated to a different geography. And strategies can become culturally outdated. Leaders who are genuine about helping their people succeed will share their strategies, but won't sanction strategies with the same timeless authority as success truths.

Some people criticize motivational speakers as purveyors of hype more than substance. Sometimes we deserve the criticism. In my early years as a motivational speaker, my enthusiasm to get people excited about the potential of their success caused me to put way too much emphasis on the trimmings of success and not enough emphasis on the core values that lead to success. I do believe that the trophies of success can ignite people's excitement. But it's teaching people the core values that lead to success that will have the most impact on helping others succeed.

If a leader wants to have the most genuine impact in the lives of followers, major on promoting the success truths that have empowered people of all backgrounds throughout history. Shouting, "This ain't rocket science," or "This is so easy a cave man could do it!" is not being genuine because success doesn't come easily. It's more genuine for a leader to say, "The challenges on the road to success are great, but the power within you is greater!" Because, that will always be true!

The late Jim Rohn is respected as one of the greatest success philosophers of our time. He stuck to promoting what he called the fundamentals. He confidently taught them knowing that the application of those truths would work for anyone, in any situation or location. Here are four of the success truths that Jim Rohn taught. They still stand even though he is no longer with us.

◆ Success is what you attract by the person you become.

◆ Develop the skills to get along with imperfect people, for even a fool can get along with perfect people.

◆ Don't join an easy crowd. You won't grow. Go where the expectations and the demands to perform and achieve are high.

◆ The ultimate reason for setting goals is to entice you to become the person it takes to achieve them.

A genuine leader loves his people enough to risk not being loved by them.

One time, I was flying back to Los Angeles airport and an associate offered to pick me up. I accepted the offer because it would give us a chance to spend quality time together on the ride home. I also suggested that he drive my vehicle to save him from using his vehicle and fuel. Upon seeing me at the baggage claim, he pulled the car up to the curbside, parked and came inside to meet me.

Anyone who is familiar with LAX knows never to leave your vehicle unattended. My associate knew it too, but he told me that he "didn't see any cops around" and figured he would be okay. I was nervous about his assumption and, sure enough, when we got back to the car, a traffic patrol officer walked up and placed a parking citation under the wiper blade. Although my associate had not seen him, the traffic patroller had seen the parking violation! Despite my associate's certainty, we got cited. But more amazing was that my associate made no effort to take responsibility for it. He never apologized and did not offer to pay the fine.

Now you are probably thinking, "Yeah what a foolish thing for your associate to do." But the point I want to make is this: After realizing that he wasn't going to remedy the situation, I swept it under the carpet telling him to not worry about it and that I would take care of it. After all, he incurred the fine while doing me a favor. That was both disingenuous and unwise on my part. In order to "not make a big thing about it," I missed an opportunity to challenge my associate about taking personal responsibility for his errors.

> Sometimes people are traveling along at great speed in the wrong direction. A leader has the responsibility to help the person turn around.

My rationale was that he didn't have much money, so it would be less of a financial hit for me. The reality was that my associate didn't have much money because he was financially irresponsible and I had just contributed to him continuing in that vein. Even though I was perplexed and mildly resentful for his actions, in the end, I didn't want to bring it up because I didn't want to risk him being upset with me. I was not a genuine leader at that point because I put my own needs to be "accepted" over his needs to learn responsibility. His life continued down a path of financial turmoil and I missed an opportunity to help him develop a lesson in financial accountability.

There is a story about a tourist who stopped his car on the road and asked a country boy how far it was to Smithsville. The country boy replied, "It's 24,000 miles the way you're heading, but if you turn around, it's just over a mile." Sometimes people are traveling along at great speed in the wrong direction. Although it may be uncomfortable to bring someone's attention to it, a leader has a responsibility to help the person turn around. A genuine leader won't sweep the destructive behaviors of their followers under the carpet to preserve the leader's likability.

Don't be afraid to address the issues that will help your followers to become leaders. Your followers may initially be irritated by you holding them accountable, but if you do so with genuine love and concern, you will win their favor in the long run.

Followership skills

There is so much written about being an effective leader but not so much is written about being an effective follower. Being a great follower should be esteemed. It might be a secondary position but it is not an inferior one. The best training for leadership comes from becoming a superb follower of a capable leader. It has even been said that you cannot become a great leader until you have learned what it takes to be a great follower. You are going to learn more about what it takes to become successful from being a prince of somebody else's mountain than being the king of your own molehill. Here are a few keys to increasing your followership skills.

Be a loyal follower.

Embrace the role of being a dynamic follower. You are not inferior, rather you are in training. Unless you first learn how to be an effective follower, you will fall short as a leader. Don't be so immature as to expect perfection from your leader. Too many people jump from following one leader to another thinking they will find the one leader who "has it all." As long as your leader is leading with moral integrity, stick with them. They deserve your absolute loyalty. Honor your leader and they will, in turn, fuel your advancement in honor of your followership.

Never make verbal commitments to your leader and then fail on delivery.

Nothing quite erodes a leader's spirit than people who over-promise and under-deliver. Leaders much prefer you to promise them nothing and then surprise them with your delivery. A genuine follower will never say, "You can count on me" and then when it comes times to deliver, all that is supplied is a bunch of excuses. Be careful of your words. Let your promises be fewer and your deliveries be greater. In other words, let your results do the speaking for you.

Never attend alone.

If your leader hosts an event or meeting, bring someone with you, or even better, bring many people with you. Arriving at a meeting with three empty seats in your car is an ineffective use of resources and is wasting an opportunity. The impact of a meeting is amplified when you experience it with people that you have invited. Even for natural introverts (of which I am one), you get more out of a meeting, and you add more energy to a meeting when you attend bringing a tribe with you.

Now to the How to: Skill

1. Commit to arriving at your leader's next meeting with all the seats in your vehicle filled. Increase your gathering skills.

2. Print out the summary of sales skills and commit them to memory.

3. Practice your selling skills by role playing at your team's meetings.

4. If you are not enrolled in an educational or personal development program that you pay for, enroll in one.

5. Do not overlook destructive traits in your followers in an attempt to preserve your leader "likability" factor. Have one "hard" conversation with a follower this week for the sake of their development and growth.

Quick FUEL: Skill

It's not a matter of "if" but rather "when" trouble comes our way. Handling trouble is a skill that every successful person has had to learn. *Stan Endicott*

All of the top achievers I know are life-long learners, looking for new skills, insights, and ideas. If they're not learning, they're not growing, not moving toward excellence. *Denis Waitley*

If money is your hope for independence you will never have it. The only real security that a man will have in this world is a reserve of knowledge, experience, and ability. *Henry Ford*

Skill and confidence are an unconquered army. *George Herbert*

Few things are impossible to diligence and skill. *Samuel Johnson*

Don't bring your need to the marketplace, bring your skill. If you don't feel well, tell your doctor, but not the marketplace. If you need money, go to the bank, but not the marketplace. *Jim Rohn*

Education is not preparation for life; education is life itself. *John Dewey*

Skill to do comes of doing. *Ralph Waldo Emerson*

'Tis God gives skill, but not without men's hands: He could not make Antonio Stradivarius violins without Antonio. *George Eliot*

Just having hope ain't going to cut it. You've got to have hope, passion and skills. *Tim Reid*

You want to find a place where, because of your skills, you can make an impact. *John McKinley*

Success Workshop: Skill

1. Do you love to learn new skills or are forced to learn new skills by changing circumstances? Rate yourself on the following scale.

Forced learner   Self motivated learner

2. What new skill have you worked on in the past six months?

_____

_____

3. What personal skills would you like to develop?

_____

_____

4. How much money do you currently invest per month for the sake of developing your skills?

_____

5. When it comes to dealing with people, what area do you need improvement?

_____

_____

6. What specific skill should your team be working on all the time?

_____

_____

7. What are the top three skills necessary for success in your enterprise?

_____

_____

_____

7. Favor

Some are satisfied to stand politely before the
portals of fortune and to await her bidding;
better those who push forward, who employ
their enterprise, who on the wings of their
worth and valor seek to embrace luck,
and to effectively gain her favor.
Baltasar Gracian

The will of a wealthy man was being read and
his relatives were listening expectantly, especially his
playboy nephew. Finally, the lawyer read: "And to my
nephew, John, whom I promised not to forget in my
will, 'Hi there, John!'"

Being on the receiving end of favor sure helps
in the quest for success. But is gaining favor something as tenuous as a rich uncle remembering you in
his will? Are there ways of attracting more favor towards you? Yes, there are ways of increasing favor
towards you, no rich uncle required!

Most of my successes can be traced back to a person extending favor towards me. I didn't do a dance for the favor, nor did I always deserve it. Yet favor flowed because I was positioned for it. Without those favors, clearly I would not be as far along the journey of success as I am. Receiving favor from someone else is certainly a factor for fueling success.

Can you succeed without anyone doing you the kindness of a favor? Perhaps. I just don't know of any successful people who don't attribute some of their success to being the recipient of an unmerited break somewhere along the line. My conclusion is that while man has the potential to be "self-made," the truth is that no one stands completely free from owing a debt of gratitude to someone who opened a door somewhere along the journey.

Among the qualities I have addressed so far, favor is the most ambiguous of them all. We benefit from favor and there is much of it out there looking for someone upon whom to land, but favor is a benefit that is largely outside of our control. You can't say, "Get out there and take some favor," like you would say "Take some responsibility!" or "Take a risk." Likewise you can say, "Increase your faith! Increase your vision! Increase your passion!" But to say "Increase your favor," really begs the question: "How?"

> While you cannot create or demand favor, you can position yourself to attract it.

You can't force people to cut you a break. So, how do you gain favor from people that would give your success journey a serendipitous boost? Here's what you need to know: While you cannot create or demand favor, you can position yourself to attract it. Commit to the following and you will increase the amount of favor that you receive.

Be the solution to other people's needs

Favor flows to those who anticipate and solve the needs of others. When you genuinely care more about the needs of the person with whom you are engaging than your own needs, you will attract more favor.

As a guest speaker at different events, I work hard to intentionally convey genuine appreciation to the brave leaders that host the event because getting people to attend meetings, no matter what size, is an enormous task. Leaders and organizers of events are well worthy of double honor. While the saying, "If you build it, they will come" sounds believable, in reality there is no such guarantee. Many of my leader friends have known what it is to host magnificent events only to pay the budget shortfall out of their own personal funds when registrations fell short.

> When the next sale determines whether your family will eat or starve, it's hard to think about putting the other person's needs above your own. But you must.

So, whenever I step onto the stage I recognize what a privilege it is. Though I work hard to deliver an inspiring message, I remind myself that these people did not come because of me. They came because someone went to the hard work of galvanizing people, organizing the event, and making personal guarantees to cover the financial shortfall if the attendance doesn't measure up to expectations. I am there as a servant. My job is to help the leaders achieve their goals in holding the event. That spirit has helped me gain the favor of many leaders and when I am blessed to be invited back, I am sure that spirit of servanthood is one of the reasons why.

Harvard trained behavioral scientist, Dr. Larry Scherwitz gives the key to increasing your favor, "Listen with regard when others talk. Give your time and energy to others; let others have their own way; do things for reasons other than furthering your own needs." Putting the needs of others before your own needs is a key to winning favor. It sounds simple, but admittedly, it's a hard key to remember when you are desperate. When the next sale determines whether your family will eat or starve, it's hard to think about putting the other person's needs above your own. But you must. Remember, favor, dignity and success flows to the person who can keep the needs of others above their own.

Be a life bringer

People who bestow favor upon others are inclined to favor those who bring life into an atmosphere. You never know who might be impacted by your countenance, so bring life and value to every environment. Don't selectively turn on your qualities when it may advantage you. Train yourself to keep your energy switch on.

Be the first to smile. Be the first to give a compliment. Be the first to volunteer your name. Be the one who inquires about what the other person is interested in. Be the first to ask for their business card. Be the first to call a few days later and leave an encouraging message. Look for little ways that you can stand out from the rest. Don't forget that in this age of electronic messaging, sending a hand-written postcard or letter can make a far greater impression than writing on someone's electronic wall.

Make it your purpose to bring light and life to other people's lives. Doing so establishes a magnetic field that attracts favor. You won't know from which direction it will come, but favor will come. For how long should you keep this up? Anyone can be momentarily vibrant. The people who experience the most favor are the ones who are continually vibrant. It is surprising to me how much favor I experience as a result of being someone's "breath of fresh air" many years before. You can create a favor momentum!

Be good at the forgotten virtues

There is an old maxim in ancient literature that says, "A person's gift makes a way for them and ushers them into the presence of kings." Yes, if you are a brilliant golfer, inventor, investor, or dress designer, you are going to gain some attention. Being great at some skill that is valued in the marketplace bodes well for the brilliant person. But don't tune out because you feel that you don't have that one incredible skill. Being good at the forgotten virtues can create as much favor as being excellent at a particular talent.

Become excellent in "life qualities" that don't require genetic gifting. Keep your word, be dependable, follow up, clean up, go the extra mile, be the first to arrive and the last to leave, the first to sign up, and the first to ask for more responsibility. Build a reputation for being a "doer" and then seek to improve that reputation.

Frankly, the world doesn't need any more brilliant and talented people over which to become enamored. The world needs more people who have the heart to encourage and inspire others to personally grow. You don't need to be great in some talent. You just need to be great at consistently doing good. Do this and favor will find you. Even the favor of kings.

Be courageous

The courageous receive more favor than others. As the Roman poet Ovid (43 B.C.) once wrote, "Fortune and love favor the brave." What are you currently doing in your life that your team would consider as brave? In his book, *You Gotta Keep Dancin'*, Tim Hansel talks about surviving a mountain climbing fall from a glacier. The physical repercussions from the accident left the vertebrae in his spine looking like a car pile up on a foggy freeway.

Doctor after doctor said there was nothing they could do and that Tim would just have to live with the pain. Tim recalls, "Without realizing it, I had gone into a stall where I was basically subduing and enduring pain. I didn't know I had another choice. I became more cautious in physical activity because one doctor told me that because my vertebrae were so unstable, if I hit a doorjamb wrong, I would become a paraplegic. The more cautiously I lived my life, the more intense the pain became."

What a powerful realization: "The more cautiously I lived my life, the more intense the pain became." When you are capable of living courageously, living cautiously won't take away your pain, but it will take away your joy and future favor.

Tim Hansel's breakthrough came when he found a doctor who agreed with the diagnosis of all the other doctors, but wrote a prescription that made a fundamental difference. He told Tim to recognize that the damage was done and the pain was to stay. Then he challenged Tim to "bite the bullet" and live to a hundred, fully and richly, to the limits of his courage and not his pain.

> "The size of your platform is directly proportional to the amount of pain you can endure."
> Craig Groeschel

Having courage is not about bungee jumping off a bridge. It's about living a life whereby people see your bravery rather than your pain.

Be kind

Dr. Norman Vincent Peale wrote, "When you become detached mentally from yourself and concentrate on helping other people with their difficulties, you will be able to cope with your own more effectively. Somehow, the act of self-giving is a personal power-releasing factor." Being kind brings favor on two levels. The first, as Dr. Peale highlights, is the way it infuses power into your ability to handle your own circumstances. The second is how kindness can actually elevate your own circumstances.

A few years ago, I was checking into a hotel in Kansas City. It was late and I was looking forward to a good night's sleep in preparation for speaking at a conference for the next few days. At the other end of the reception desk was a lady wearing a bandanna on her head. Her young son sat in a nearby chair in the lobby. The woman had experienced the misfortune of leaving her car lights on and consequently her car battery was completely drained. She was asking the hotel staff whether the hotel had a car battery cart whereby she could get a jump start. Not having such a unit, the hotel manager offered to call a towing company to come out and give her a jump start. The towing company was indeed willing to help, at their normal fee of fifty dollars. He turned to the lady and asked if that would be okay.

> You could sense her despair as she gathered her son and walked out into the cold night air.

I could see the woman's countenance fall. It was obviously fifty dollars that she did not have. It wasn't hard for me to notice that the bandanna that the lady was wearing was covering the effects of chemotherapy treatment. She motioned to the manager not to worry and she returned to her son who was almost asleep in the chair. You could sense her despair as she gathered her son and walked out into the cold night air.

As the hotel receptionist handed me my room key, I handed over fifty dollars and asked the manager to call the towing company back. Then I headed to my room. About twenty minutes later, the phone in my room rang. The hotel receptionist asked if I could bring my bags and return to the lobby. In the lobby, I was met by the hotel manager who explained, "Sir, we wanted to thank you for your kindness towards the lady and her son. I see that you are staying with us for three days, so we would like to put you in the presidential suite for the duration of your stay. Is that okay with you?"

One act of kindness led to another. The lady and her son were happily on their way home and I was on my way to the presidential suite. Kindness doesn't guarantee favor, but it positions you for it. Right now, so many people are fully drained. What can you do, or better yet, what can you and your team do to make a difference?

Be generous

Generosity in its purest form is being generous to those who could never repay you or return the favor. John Bunyan said, "You have not lived today until you have done something for someone who can never repay you." That's the spirit that ultimately positions you in the flow of favor—both giving and receiving.

Develop the personal quality of generosity. Flood the world with as much of your brand of generosity as possible and it will return to you. Favor flows more to those who are inclined towards giving it, rather than those actively seeking to receive it.

Challenge yourself to commit actions of generosity every day. Be generous by lifestyle. For the price of some creative thinking, generosity rarely requires much money. Be generous by habit. It will do something to your persona that attracts favor.

Be confident in your goal

Roman philosopher Seneca said it best, "To the person who does not know where he wants to go there is no favorable wind." Having a strong sense of purpose attracts support to the fulfillment of the purpose. People like to get behind those who know where they are going and are confident in their objective. Where are you headed? What is it that you stand for? What is it that you are fighting for? Having concise answers to these questions, both as an individual and as a team, will increase your attractiveness to like minded people.

We are constantly being asked, "What do you do?" Yet, we often fudge around looking for the words to say. Often we never give the same answer twice. Establish your purpose in one short sentence, memorize it, and train yourself to convey it confidently in any situation. Don't rush your words, express them thoughtfully and deliberately. When asked what I do, my answer is simple, "I help people increase their personal productivity and results." Of course that is just the tip of the iceberg but that is just enough to resonate with the right people. Your vision, well articulated, will garner the enthusiasm of others who relate to your vision.

Be positive by predisposition

Predispose yourself to be positive about people. Nothing repels favor like a critical spirit towards others. Yes, there are people who deserve criticism, but you can't afford the price of being the one who dispenses it. Being critical can start out as a valid response to an injustice, but it too easily morphs into a disposition. Our human spirit has a natural proclivity to project ill-thoughts into a relationship when things don't go our way. When we start to cooperate with that inclination, favor stops flowing in our direction. Reverse the tendency by resisting the temptation. Even if a person deserves a dose of criticism, don't you be the one to serve it up. It's not worth what it will do to your spirit.

Many years ago, I wrote this poem to help remind myself to be positive towards people. I still recite it to myself—often! It recalibrates my spirit and restores me to a place of attracting favor.

Think the Best

Think the best of life and people
Don't waste time thinking feeble
Make your mind behave the way
Of who you want to be one day
Think success before the fact
Let it shine through word and act
Visualize who you will be
Thinking shapes your destiny

Wes Beavis

It's harder to regulate the receiving of favor in your life, than regulating the increase of faith and vision. Yet, favor is an important ingredient in the success mix. Favor flows to and from people every day. So seek to employ every means of positioning yourself within that flow. Give favor and position yourself to receive it as well.

Now to the How to: Favor

1. Live each day with an expectation of being within the flow of favor. Remind yourself daily that you are excellent at bestowing favor and worthy of receiving favor.

2. Write to your team leader and express gratitude for being the recipient of their time and favor.

3. Commit to putting the needs of others before your own.

4. Make a list of people you want to give favor. Work through the list making a note of responses. Share the reactions and responses at your next team meeting.

5. Work out a concise and interesting response to the question, "What is it that you do?" Practice your answer so that it flows naturally and confidently.

Quick FUEL: Favor

The moment one definitely commits oneself, providence moves too. A whole stream of events issues from the decision, raising in one's favor all manner of unforeseen incidents, meetings and material assistance, which no man could have dreamt would have come his way. *William Hutchinson Murray*

Did you ever observe to whom the accidents happen? Chance favors only the prepared mind.
Louis Pasteur

He who finds fortune on his side should go briskly ahead, for she is wont to favor the bold.
Baltasar Gracian

To do a great job today is the best way to gain favor tomorrow. *Stan Endicott*

Favor and honor sometimes fall more fitly on those who do not desire them. *Titus Livius*

Do not offer a compliment and ask a favor at the same time. A compliment that is charged for is not valuable. *Mark Twain*

I am prejudiced in favor of him who, without impudence, can ask boldly. He has faith in humanity, and faith in himself. No one who is not accustomed to giving grandly can ask nobly and with boldness.
Johann Kaspar Lavater

Good presentations find favor. Bad ones discover critics. *Arthur Tugman*

The person who receives the most favors is the one who knows how to return them.
Publilius Syrus

If we do what is necessary, all the odds are in our favor. *Charles Buxton*

That man is worthless who knows how to receive a favor, but not how to return one.
Titus Maccius Plautus

Success Workshop: Favor

1. If fortune favors the bold, I consider myself at this point on the boldness scale.

Bold on occasions   Always bold

2. Think of the major breakthroughs in your life. Did they come as the result of someone's favor? List some breakthroughs along with the person whose favor made it possible.

_____

_____

_____

_____

_____

_____

3. Was there anything that you did to position your-self for the favor you listed above? Explain.

_____

_____

_____

_____

4. Name someone in your life at the moment to whom you could show some extra kindness.

_____

What could you do for this person?

_____

_____

5. What three qualities could you develop that would increase the potential for you to receive favor from others?

_____

_____

_____

8. Fight

There is some good in this world,
and it's worth fighting for.
J.R.R. Tolkien

███▀█▀█▀

On January 8th, 2004, Anne Hjelle went mountain bike riding with her friend, Debi Nicholls. They were totally unaware that on the same trail they were riding, another mountain bike rider had just been attacked and killed by a mountain lion. Little did they know, the same mountain lion would come back for more.

Anne had established a slight lead over Debi as they rode the rugged trails of Whiting Ranch Wilderness Park in Southern California. It was a lead that protected Debi from being the next victim. Anne recalls seeing a flash of brown, reddish fur in her peripheral vision. For a split second, she thought that she had startled a deer which were known to sometimes graze near the bike trail. Her logical thought was quickly dismissed as a fully grown male mountain lion sank its teeth into Anne's neck, forcefully sending her careening off her bike and landing in a ravine. Without warning, Anne was in the fight of her life.

The lion repeatedly bit into Anne's neck and face in an effort to gain just the right grip in order to sever Anne's spinal cord, paralyze her, and succeed in making the kill. But Anne's bike helmet stopped the lion from being able to obtain the perfect bite that would have instantly ended her life.

By this time, Debi joined the fight. She entered a tug-of-war with the mountain lion. As the lion dragged Anne further down the ravine, Debi clutched Anne's left ankle and vowed, "I'm not going to let you die." While Debi was trying to wrestle Anne from the lion's jaws, Anne was praying and punching the lion in the head. But by that stage, the lion was in the "kill trance" and no amount of punching, wrestling or screaming was making the slightest difference to the lion's intentions.

> "Hjelle realized that if she survived, she would be disfigured. For a split second, she wondered if she'd be better off dead."
>
> Los Angeles Times

Debi, with every strain of muscle that her slight frame could offer, was fighting to pull Anne uphill and out of the lion's death grip. The stronger mountain lion was pulling Anne downhill and ripping the left side of her face off at the same time. The fight was hopelessly lopsided. When the lion clasped its jaws around her throat, Anne blacked out.

Mike Castellano, 41, one of two men that came to the cyclists' rescue, told the LA Times: "I have never seen anything like this —it was a tug of war between the mountain lion trying to drag her down the ravine by her face and the cycling companion who had her by the legs." www.timesonline.co.uk

Then two factors came into play that swung the odds into Anne and Debi's favor. The first factor was that another group of mountain bikers happened to be riding along the same trail. When they heard the fighting and screaming, they jumped off their bikes and started throwing rocks at the lion. The second factor was that the lion, in dragging Anne down into the ravine, had backed itself into a tree. In that moment the lion, recognizing the presence of more people and being backed into a tree, released its grip on Anne. It retreated a little distance, lurking for an opportune moment to attack again.

Someone in the second group of riders had called the 911emergency hotline. Nineteen minutes later, a rescue team arrived. A helicopter hovered above them sending radio communications to the rescue team below in the ravine. The paramedics positioned themselves between Anne and the moun-tain lion. The helicopter pilots monitored the position of the lion and informed the medics that it was prowl-ing right behind them, looking to attack again. The medic who was administering an intravenous needle into Anne's arm, had to keep his hands from shaking. Getting a needle into Anne's vein with a threatening lion lurking behind them was a miracle in itself.

A rescue helicopter airlifted Anne to Mission Hospital in Orange County. Having survived the initial fight for her life, the next fight was about to begin. The surgeons operating on Anne said that it was as if someone had opened up the entire left side of her face, thrown in a couple of handfuls of dirt and then closed the flap again. The damage was immense and the likelihood of infection was extremely high. Painstakingly, the doctors cleansed, stitched and hoped that Anne could fight the infection, possible rabies, and the effects of massive blood loss.

Winning that battle, Anne was to fight the next battle. Life was forever changed from the way she had known it prior to the attack. Even after recovery, there was no returning to what life had been. She knew that the recovery process would be long. Her husband, James, would be under enormous pressure as caretaker and provider. Anne knew that James could handle it and would not waiver, but she grieved that his life would be so impacted.

Physically, Anne no longer looked the same. Adjusting to the drastic change to her physical appearance was another battle. Every time Anne looked in the mirror, she had to reformulate her expectations. The familiar face was gone. The process of incorporating her new, scarred look into her mind was both difficult and wearisome. Yet, battle by battle, Anne kept fighting and winning.

There was yet another challenge ahead for Anne and James. Having survived the life-changing trauma of a lion attack, Anne was reluctantly thrust into the media spotlight. Every major media outlet wanted to interview her. From breakfast shows to *Larry King Live*, the invitations came. Although she preferred to be more "behind the scenes," Anne figured that if her experience could help others gain courage, she was willing to tell her story and speak of her faith.

In reflecting upon her ordeal, Anne told me that when the lion had its jaws clamped onto her neck and when she realized that her face had been ripped away, it became as much an emotional fight as physical. She knew that it would be easy to give up, to stop fighting, and let the lion have its way. Anne said that there was an amazing mental dialogue that was going on in her head—even as the lion ripped into her body. Anne recalls profoundly, "It was the mental patterns that I developed day to day that kicked in when I was in the fight for my life. I believed life was worth the fight and so I did."

> "It was a miracle that, with her face so badly damaged, Hjelle's eye was unharmed."
> CBS News

Now, James and Anne's message to others is about developing the best perspective in any given situation. Anne says, "Instead of focusing on the scars, I think about how incredible it is that I still have 20/20 vision in both eyes." In speaking with me recently, Anne said, "Wes, people have more fight in them than they realize. People have said to me, 'I could never go through what you went through.' And my response is, 'You don't realize how strong you really are!'"

Anne's friend, Debi Nicholls, fought the lion in a brutal tug-of-war.

Anne on the bike trails of Aliso and Wood canyons in Laguna Beach, Southern California.

Anne sustained forty deep bite wounds to her neck and her face was pieced together using more than 200 stitches and staples.

Anne with her husband, James.

"Sure, I look different than I used to,
but I feel like the same person inside.
Even on days when I lacked self-confi-
dence, I chose to put on a smile. I acted
strong when I didn't feel strong—and
before long, I was strong!" Anne Hjelle

photos provided courtesy of www.annehjelle.com

Always be the fighter!

You must be a fighter if you want to succeed because in life you don't get what you deserve, nor do you get what is fair. You get what you fight for. Don't think that people succeed because they were lucky and just met the right person at the right time. It may look like that from the outside but it was their willingness to keep fighting that ultimately led them to success.

Reaching your goals will be a daily battle. Margaret Thatcher once said, "You may have to fight a battle more than once to win it." That is so true, especially when the first battlefront is for your mind. As Sally Kempton said, "It is hard to fight an enemy who has outposts in your head." Once you have the daily battle for your thinking won, then you are armed to fight the inevitable dragons that are between you and your goal. Achieving success will be a battle. That is guaranteed. So the only question is, "Will the fighter show up every day to conquer that battle?"

Success doesn't favor the lucky; it favors the fighter. Will you fight rejection and overcome it on a daily basis? For not every day will greet you with the right mix of emotions or circumstances. Will you fight the blues and the blah's? The fighter within you can. Will you fight to be productive? Will you fight the human propensity to fritter away precious time? Will you fight for better results and keep fighting for your dream?

In the quest to inspire Britain not to lose heart in the darkest hour of World War II, Winston Churchill declared, "We shall defend our island, whatever the cost may be, we shall fight on the beaches, we shall fight on the landing grounds, we shall fight in the fields and in the streets, we shall fight in the hills; we shall never surrender."

Can you, even in your darkest hour, declare with Churchill passion, "I shall defend my vision, I shall take responsibility, whatever the cost may be, I will fight the challenges, I will fight the temptation to be negative, I shall fight apathy, I will fight to be guided by my dreams and not my circumstances, I will fight to improve every day, for the sake of a better future for everyone, for the sake of leaving this earth having given more than what I have taken, I shall never NEVER surrender!" In the face of despair, may that be the battle cry that fuels your spirit to press on.

People who live extraordinary lives are simply ordinary people who decide to fight for something better than ordinary and they never surrender. You don't need to be attacked by a mountain lion to discover how strong you are. You are stronger than you realize. Dream a big dream and let that revolutionize your life and your world. Fire up your fighting spirit. Fuel up every day for the battle. Never surrender. Yes, the challenges on the road to success are great, but the power in you is greater! Get out there and fight for a better life and it will inevitably be yours.

Now to the How to: Fight

1. Identify yourself as a fighter who never gives up on the dream of a better life.

2. Write to your leader and let them know that you are grateful that they never gave up during tough times.

3. Write out your version of Winston Churchill's "We will never surrender" speech. Personalize it to your life and your dream.

4. When faced with seemingly insurmountable odds, state your name and follow it with the words:
 "[Your name] you are stronger than you realize."
Repeat it several times as you press on in faith, proving that the statement is true.

Quick FUEL: Fight

You cannot run away from weakness; you must some time fight it out or perish; and if that be so, why not now, and where you stand? *Robert Louis Stevenson*

We are twice armed if we fight with faith. *Plato*

While women weep, as they do now, I'll fight; while children go hungry, as they do now I'll fight; while men go to prison, in and out, in and out, as they do now, I'll fight; while there is a drunkard left, while there is a poor lost girl upon the streets, while there remains one dark soul without the light of God, I'll fight, I'll fight to the very end! *William Booth*

What counts is not necessarily the size of the dog in the fight—it's the size of the fight in the dog.
Dwight D. Eisenhower

Victory is always possible for the person who refuses to stop fighting. *Napoleon Hill*

You can lay down and die, or you can get up and fight, but that's it—there's no turning back. *Jon English*

By far the most dangerous foe we have to fight is apathy—indifference from whatever cause, not from a lack of knowledge, but from carelessness, from absorption in other pursuits, from a contempt bred of self satisfaction. *William Osler*

Who has a harder fight than he who is striving to overcome himself. *Thomas Kempis*

If you fight you might lose, if you don't you have already lost. *Bertolt Brecht*

Every soldier must know, before he goes into battle, how the little battle he is to fight fits into the larger picture, and how the success of his fighting will influence the battle as a whole.
Bernard Law Montgomery

All endeavor calls for the ability to tramp the last mile, shape the last plan, endure the last hours toil. The fight to the finish spirit is the one characteristic we must possess if we are to face the future as finishers.
Henry David Thoreau

Success Workshop: Fight

1. When in the heat of the battle, what is your natural tendency—towards flight or fight? Rate yourself on the following scale.

Flight   Fight

2. Recall a time in your life when you stood your ground and stared down the challenge that was facing you.

_____

_____

3. Recall a time when you gave up—took flight—and in retrospect wished you had stood your ground and kept fighting.

_____

_____

4. Name three people in your life that you admire for their fighting qualities.

_____

_____

_____

5. For what cause are you willing to stay in the fight and never surrender?

_____

_____

_____

_____

Receive the Wes Word!

www.WesBeavis.com

Photo: Mark Lydell

Wes Beavis has been motivating audiences
around the world for over twenty years.
His passion is helping people to increase
their personal productivity and results.

If you would like Wes Beavis to speak
at your event, he would love to do so.
Contact him at:

www.WesBeavis.com/contact/book.asp